THE PENGUIN POETS

RELATIONS

Born in 1925 in New Hampshire, Philip Booth grew up
there and in Maine, where he now lives in the house that
has belonged to his family for five generations. He was
educated at Dartmouth and Columbia, and has long
taught in the Syracuse University Creative Writing Pro-
gram.

Philip Booth's poems have appeared in a wide variety
of journals, textbooks, and anthologies for over thirty
years, and have been translated into French, Italian, Por-
tuguese, Finnish, and Dutch. His books of poetry in-
clude *Letter from a Distant Land, The Islanders, Weathers
and Edges, Margins, Available Light,* and *Before Sleep.* He
has been awarded grants by the Guggenheim Founda-
tion, the Rockefeller Foundation, the National Institute
of Arts and Letters, and the National Endowment for the
Arts. He has most recently been honored by election as
a Fellow of the Academy of American Poets.

RELATIONS

SELECTED POEMS 1950-1985

PHILIP BOOTH

PENGUIN BOOKS

PENGUIN BOOKS
Viking Penguin Inc., 40 West 23rd Street,
New York, New York 10010, U.S.A.
Penguin Books Ltd, Harmondsworth,
Middlesex, England
Penguin Books Australia Ltd, Ringwood,
Victoria, Australia
Penguin Books Canada Limited, 2801 John Street,
Markham, Ontario, Canada L3R 1B4
Penguin Books (N.Z.) Ltd, 182–190 Wairau Road,
Auckland 10, New Zealand

First published in 1986 in simultaneous hardcover and
paperback editions by Viking Penguin Inc.
Published simultaneously in Canada

The poems in Sections I–VI of this collection originally ap-
peared in *The American Poetry Review, Antaeus, The Antioch Re-
view, The Atlantic Monthly, Choomia, Columbia Forum, The
Distinctive Voice, Field, Harper's Magazine, The Hudson Review,
Kayak, The Kenyon Review, The London Magazine, The Missouri
Review, The Nation, New Orleans Poetry Journal, The New Repub-
lic, The New York Review of Books, The New Yorker, Ploughshares,
Poetry, Poetry Northwest, Quest, Salmagundi, The Saturday Re-
view, Shenandoah, Syntax, The Syracuse 10 Magazine, Tri-
Quarterly, The Virginia Quarterly Review,* and in the author's
earlier books *Letter from a Distant Land, The Islanders, Weathers
and Edges, Margins, Available Light,* and *Before Sleep,* published
by Viking Penguin Inc.

Grateful acknowledgment is made for permission to reprint two
excerpts from *The Unquiet Grave* by Cyril Connolly, © 1981 by
Deirdre Levi, reprinted by permission of Persea Books, New
York, N.Y.

The Acknowledgments on page 260 constitute an extension of
this copyright page.

LIBRARY OF CONGRESS CATALOGING IN PUBLICATION DATA
Booth, Philip E.
  Relations: selected poems, 1950–1985.
  I. Title.
PS3503.O532A6 1986   811'.54   86-923
ISBN 0 14 058.560 5

Printed in the United States of America by
R. R. Donnelley & Sons Company, Harrisonburg, Virginia
Set in Garamond No. 3
Design by Ann Gold

CONTENTS

RELATIONS

*Not until we are lost . . . do we
begin to find ourselves, and realize
where we are and the infinite extent
of our relations.*

—Thoreau

*Underneath the rational and
voluntary world is the involuntary,
impulsive, integrated world, the
world of Relation in which
everything is one . . .*

—Palinurus

I.

ADAM

I take thee now to be no other
than you are. In the raw weather
of Northeast storms, in summer meadows
run with only the seabirds' shadows,

I risk my naked and imperfect praise.
From noon to sunlit moon, the days
make ceremony of my quick desire.
Wave by wave, the gray stone shore

diminishes to sand, the known coast
ebbs: and we stand watching, crest
on blue and whitecap crest, who search
still for a tidal lovers' beach.

Yet never do quivering lovers touch
the secret place they join to reach;
at flood between them, love divides,
as barred islands by spring tides.

So must we, Eve, content ourselves
how close we came. At equinox, our lives
are time enough to love again,
between the loon call and the rain.

And there is world enough. I claim
this coast by giving it a name;
I give you this calm morning
as the first, without storm warning

in the cirrus sky. Fish and seal,
crab and beach-pea, breed original
in my mind: heather, starfish forms,
are mine. I love you by the terms

I make to give you. I wake to call
the osprey, tern, the slow-winged gull,
say all the sea's grave names, and build
with words this beach that is the world.

FIRST LESSON

Lie back, daughter, let your head
be tipped back in the cup of my hand.
Gently, and I will hold you. Spread
your arms wide, lie out on the stream
and look high at the gulls. A dead-
man's-float is face down. You will dive
and swim soon enough where this tidewater
ebbs to the sea. Daughter, believe
me, when you tire on the long thrash
to your island, lie up, and survive.
As you float now, where I held you
and let go, remember when fear
cramps your heart what I told you:
lie gently and wide to the light-year
stars, lie back, and the sea will hold you.

SHAG

Under the slow heron,
flip tern, and swung gull,
six black shags run on
the water, each duck skull

filled with weathervane
thought. Toward east wind
they take off on the run,
splashing until the shag mind

tells spent feet to retract.
Then the seventh shag,
straggling, begins to react.
His head bobs. The fog

closing in, he raises
himself on gargoyle wings,
drops again, then rises
and runs as he bangs

the sea on all fours.
Slowly, then faster, he skims
the dark fir shores.
Momentarily, he seems

to join the first flight.
But he shoots away,
shaglike, his thought flat
black. All shags fly

low. Ornithologists know
more: the perhaps why
and improbable how
of shag flight. They

call them cormorants,
or latinize the North name.
I row slow in the dense
weather. This is Maine;

and I slap the split port oar
of my leaking skiff,
drifting among the fir
islands, the seabirds, as if

on vacation from knowledge:
six black shags, shagging;
August fog, me, a Maine ledge,
and the seventh shag, lagging.

VERMONT: INDIAN SUMMER

Unseasonable
as bees in April,
rime in May,
or Orion high
in June,
          days lost
somewhere in August,
green days, dun,
return at noon
as numb-winged wasps
swim in the lapse
of weather:
                    sun
and weathervane
are still; the cows
wait, hillside crows
caw down to barn
the first-frost burn
of sumac, maple,
and sideyard apple.

The sky is halo-
hazed, barn and silo
smell of baled hay,
corn-crib, and dry
harvest days;
                    days,
goldenrod days:
and the dazzled wasps
climb numb in the lapse
of weather, lost
in what cannot last,
wings struck dumb,
in this other summer,
summer twice come.

IGHTSONG

Beside you,
lying down at dark,
my waking fits your sleep.

Your turning
flares the slow-banked fire
between our mingled feet,

and there,
curved close and warm
against the nape of love,

held there,
who holds your dreaming
shape, I match my breathing

to your breath;
and sightless, keep my hand
on your heart's breast, keep

nightwatch
on your sleep to prove
there is no dark, nor death.

NORTH

North is weather, winter, and change:
a wind-shift, snow, and how ice ages
shape the moraine of a mountain range.

At tree line the chiseled ledges
are ragged to climb; wind-twist trees
give way to the thrust of granite ridges,

peaks reach through abrasive centuries
of rain. The worn grain, the sleet-cut,
is magnified on blue Northwest days

where rock slides, like rip-tide, break out
through these geologic seas. Time
in a country of hills is seasonal light:

alpenglow, Northern lights, and tame
in October: Orion, cold hunter of stars.
Between what will be and was, rime

whites the foothill night and flowers
the rushes stilled in black millpond ice.
The dark, the nightfall temperatures

are North, and the honk of flyway geese
high over valley sleep. The woodland
is evergreen, ground pine, spruce,

and deadwood hills at the riverbend.
Black bear and mink fish beaver streams
where moose and caribou drink; beyond

the forests there are elk. Snowstorms
breed North like arctic birds that swirl
downhill, and in a blind wind small farms

are lost. At night the close cold is still,
the tilt world returns from sun to ice.
Glazed lichen is North, and snowfall

at five below. North is where rockface
and hoarfrost are formed with double grace:
love is twice warm in a cold place.

DESIGN

Around the tree
they won't outgrow,

plowing with
cold feet, warm breath,

to tramp a wreath
or trace the path

of their amaze-
ment in wet snow,

my children wander
at cross-purposes,

cross-sectioning
the marvelous yard.

Lost in laughter
where they blunder

kneedeep
in geometry,

neither daughter
half supposes

that while they sleep,
the tree, the yard,

the crystal maze
of quartered ring

and staggered line,
will freeze, freeze

hard: design
within design.

LETTER FROM A DISTANT LAND

> *I, on my side, require of every writer,*
> *first or last, a simple and sincere*
> *account of his own life . . . some such*
> *account as he would send to his*
> *kindred from a distant land . . .*
> —Thoreau, *Walden*

Henry, my distant kin,
                I live halfway,
halfway between an airfield and your pond,
halfway within the house I moved to buy
by borrowing. On transcendental ground,
come south from colder hills and early dusk,
we claim two acres of uneven land.
Alone now, sitting at my birch-plank desk,
I see an acre out these wide new windows:
my wife cuts brush, two small girls both risk
a foot in appletrees. Across the meadows,
the alder swamp, an ash grove not yet green,
a pair of jets outrace their double shadows.
We do not look up. A grosbeak in the pine
pecks under wing, the shy hen pheasant leaves
her nibbled sumac for our scattered grain.
With rabbits, too, we share uncertain lives;
not quiet or desperate, we measure man
by how he lives and what he most believes.
I am half teacher, half-week chopping blow-down
for our fire, half-time professing words
to warm new minds with what my heart has known.
My classes are good failures. Afterwards,
I change clothes, moult my partial self,
and walk completed through the open woods.
Behind the grillwork branches where I half
confess, the chapel that I most attend
is choired by migratory birds; I loaf
within the absolution of the wind.
My thought is swiftest when my feet are slow,
but far abroad I own a spendthrift mind.
My Spanish grandfather, a tall man, knew

his knighthood from a book. So, pastoral
beside a fire, do I come slowly to know
you, odd uncle of my wakeful, still,
and secret dawns. My least experiments
with seed, like yours with a dried apple, fail;
the weeds, slugs, borers, grow as dense
as crows. I own a herd dog, but no sheep;
my cultivation is, like learning, chance.
Slack puritan I am, I let my garden shape
itself with skunks. I'm halfway, halfway only;
there are midnights when I do not sleep.

The quick night-fighters' sudden thunder shakes
this house awake. Escaped from every weather,
making prey of man, they are great sharks
with silver fins that foul the ocean air.
Propelled by jets of flame fired through their vents,
they school a noisy mile Northeast of here,
guided by blind pilots, and by governments.
A war ago, I flew myself. Now, bound
to these two acres, I owe the several debts
a lonely conscience knows. I love this land
by the salt sweat it costs to own it whole.
My birthday was a bucksaw, I still defend
the new growth with an ax: the trees I fell
need cutting to let the hardwood grow. I chop
at the lush swamp, hack down the summer jungle
rich with flies. You know how fires earned chip
by chip are warmest. Still, you could not guess
the shapes of proved destruction: chain saws rape
a virgin stand to stumps; raw foremen boss
more horsepower in a fleet of airfield trucks
than Concord ever stabled. Machines as murderous
as mad bulls gore the land. Where stacked cornshocks
stood last fall, an orange oil tank flaws
the spring; girders bloom with concrete blocks.
So far, your Concord has seen four more wars.
Vegetables are high. The streets are filled
with tourists; cheap people in expensive cars
patrol the Sunday roads. An acre sold
in 1849 sells now two hundred times

the price. Lexington is houses sprawled
on desert-dusty streets with fertile names.
The arrogant inherit lust. Everywhere,
thick rows of sportsmen fish polluted streams,
or hunt the posted woods of their own fear.
Overhead, the tight-paired jets write
cryptic warnings on the thin blue air.

Too close to earth to show to those who scan
the sky for enemy, I walked last week
beyond the impulse caught on any radar screen.
In windworn March, halfway to dawn, I woke
to feel the growing day: the wind light North-
north-west, the morning luminous, a streak
of cloud between the sunward-turning earth
and yesterday's last stars. A rebel drummer
called me like the crows. The cross-lots path
I walked was wet with melting frost, a rumor
of frogs thawed the swamp, and toward town
I heard the hard first whack of a hammer.
A casual pilgrim to the phoebe's tune,
I whistled down the distant land where you
(this same month's end) tramped out to cut white pine
with Alcott's borrowed ax. Your Walden, now,
is still half yours: a summer swimmers' beach
corrupts the eastern bank, the sun-up view,
but you, who would be saint in a formal church,
are honored still on the farther shores, preserved
in the commonwealth of hemlock, elm, and birch.
Your hut is marked by stone, the pond was saved
by taxes for a public park. Emerson's
strict laws of compensation have reserved
a parking space for Sunday lovers; beer cans
drift where you knelt soberly to drink,
and small boys smoke like truant puritans.
Such is August on the swimmers' bank,
but not my sharp March dawn. Between ice-out
and spring, I walk in time to hear the honk
of two stray geese, the song of a white-throat
soloing after his mate in your celibate woods.
That song is still the same; shadowy trout

rise like the swift perfection of your words,
the backyard journal of your human praise
is proved in the red oaks' blood-dark buds.
I like to think how animals would freeze
to see your stick, your crooked genius, poke
the leafy underbrush: until you froze
yourself, and all the thicket woodcock, duck,
and small scared beasts of Walden's shore
turned curious. Here, between the dark
and sudden milktrain day, halfway from fear,
halfway to spring, I say these natural names
to honor you as poet of the turning year.
Beside the ministry of waves, the times
of men are seasons, windfall seeds that spill
toward fruit: the perfect globe or wormy shames
of Adam. All poets climb back Eden's hill
within their own back yard. Woods and pond
were your recovery of the crop that's possible,
a harvest of good words grown from the land
that brings the whole world home. I cultivate
a different orchard, pruning under the sound
of probable war. The day's first silver jet
reflects first sunlight where I turn away
from Walden, turn, stop, look back, and start
again. Up the bank, I cross the highway
where a skunk got lost in headlights: traffic-
flat, his flowering intestines lie halfway
in sun. This new March day is sweetened thick
with death. But when was any season less?
You felt the cold fall snap of John Brown's neck,
owned a winter conscience, smelled slavery's grass-
fire torch the long dry land to civil war,
from Bull Run to Savannah to the Wilderness.
Distant from that history as we are,
the good, the brave, are no more a majority
than when you walked this far spring shore.
Man, by his human nature, is not free;
but where his wildness is alive to swamp
and hill, he learns to live most naturally.
Still, a saunterer must make his camp
in strange unholy lands, begging alms

and passage for belief. I take no stump
except for liberty to listen to the elms,
to walk the cold wood, to sleep on bedrock
thought, and to try some winter psalms.
A century from where your wisdom struck
its temporary camp, I cross the middleground
toward hope. At home beneath both oak
and jet, praising what I halfway understand,
I walk this good March morning out
to say my strange love in a distant land.

STORM IN A FORMAL GARDEN

Where my struck mother stays,
she wakes to thunderstorms
of doubt. Squalls blacken
her bright-surfaced dreams,
and she stands coldly shaken,
lost in the dripping trees.

The weather shuts and opens:
horizon lightning traps
her in a quick exposure
of old fears; she trips
and rises twice unsure.
No one knows how it happens.

Where my dark mother waits
for sun, the wet slate sky
builds prison thunderheads,
and she, mired in anxiety,
must bear the drumroll nights
struck mute by what she dreads.

Her numb-mouthed silences
are desperate prayer, or else
the panic count from flash
to thunderclap. Impulse
fires her woman flesh,
and fevers her thin balances.

Miles from where my mother
falls, in that rank formal
garden that I bend
to weed, the wrens chirp normal
pleasure on the wind,
wrens scale the turning weather.

Weeds like conscience clog
my rake. My mother craves
more love than any son

can give. And I, with leaves
jammed on a sharpened tine,
sweat where my two hearts tug.

Dreams from her, I wake
beyond my mother's hope
and will. Beyond the son
I was, and the thunder's shape,
I clear the overgrown
last path my heart must rake.

HERON

In the copper marsh
I saw a stilted heron
wade the tidal wash

and I, who caught no fish,
thought the grass barren
and that jade inlet harsh

until the quick-billed splash
of the long-necked heron
fulfilled my hunter's wish.

Then in the rising rush
of those great wings, far on
I saw the herring flash

and drop. And the dash
of lesser wings in the barren
marsh flew through my flesh.

CHART 1203
PENOBSCOT BAY AND APPROACHES

Whoever works a storm to windward, sails
in rain, or navigates in island fog,
must reckon from the slow swung lead, from squalls

on cheek; must bear by compass, chart, and log.
Parallels are ruled from compass rose
to known red nun: but still the landfall leg

risks set of tide, lost buoys, and breakers' noise
on shore where no shore was. Whoever plots
his homing on these Eastward islands knows

how Sou'west smoke obscures the sunny charts,
how gulls cry on a numberless black spar.
Where North is West of North, not true, he pilots

best who feels the coast for standpipe, spire,
tower, or stack, who owns local knowledge of shoal
or ledge, whose salt nose smells the spruce shore.

Where echoes drift, where the blind groundswell
clangs an iron bell, his fish-hook hand
keeps steady on the helm. He weathers rainsquall,

linestorm, fear, who bears away from the sound
of sirens wooing him to the cape's safe lee.
He knows the ghostship bow, the sudden headland

immanent in fog; but where rocks wander, he
steers down the channel that his courage
dredges. He knows the chart is not the sea.

THE SECOND NOON

*In my religion all believers would
stop work at sundown and have a
drink together "pour chasser la honte
du jour." This would be taken in
remembrance of the first sunset when
man must have thought the
oncoming night would prove eternal.*
  —Palinurus (Cyril Connolly),
    The Unquiet Grave

New to light that first noon,
they stand blind in the sun's meridian,
and own no sight, but hang their heads down
from that glare and first heat
until, as the day grows cool,
their accustomed eyes can open,
and they recognize the original shadows
leaning out from their feet.

Asking that afternoon nothing,
they worship the doubled forms who swim
before them onto the streaming meadows.
Grown tall at last to turn
questions, they face behind them,
full West, and—stumbling blind
beyond guesses of dawn—are pressed
into the aggregate shadows.

They wake to a slivered moon
that first night, to a sky wet with stars,
and in that world cannot believe
they see. And will not see
(as light from love revolves)
until, as their shadows come home
foot by foot, they learn to look not to the sun
but full, at high noon, to themselves.

WAS A MAN

Was a man, was a two-
faced man, pretended
he wasn't who he was,
who, in a men's room,
faced his hung-over
face in a mirror hung
over the towel rack.
The mirror was cracked.
Shaving close in that
looking glass, he nicked
his throat, bled blue
blood, grabbed a new
towel to patch the wrong
scratch, knocked off
the mirror and, facing
himself, almost intact,
in final terror hung
the wrong face back.

IF IT COMES

If it comes
to that, go
to bed late,
so, if you
have to wait
without sleep,
you can see
the luminous
dial, and keep
watch on your
self-winding
pulse. Words bug
the least light,
and full-moon
animals, out
to shuttle
the dark, drag
a trapped leg
through the rose
bed. Last night
was the same:
the same noise,
the slow night-
lock rattle,
and no one
there. Finding
yourself where
bat wings swim
the blank sky,
where owls dive
to echo
your own dark
question, yes,
you must go
to bed late:
so, if for
once, you have

enough warning,
enough to break
out, from what
pass as dreams,
you will wake,
if it comes,
near morning.

THE TOWER

Strangers ask,
always, how tall
it is. Taller,
the natives say,
than any other.
Watching it sway,
lightly, in a brisk
wind, you believe
them and feel,
well, smaller
than you once
did, or would have,
even had they woken
somebody's father,
who remembers
every specification,
they say, having fought
against this location,
in the last elections
before it was built.
It is enough
to see it, canted
over you, as
you approach
the strange base:
a cement stilt
set in a rough
patch of marsh;
on that, a ball
with numbers
etched on it,
perhaps a date,
on which the steel
frame, in one
brave unbroken
line, seems to stretch
for heaven itself,

in three diminishing
sections. The balance
is fantastic,
or seems so, until
you recall the elastic
web of guy wires
that, slanted
beyond you, support
the tower in nine
equal directions.
The local women,
hanging their wash
on a wet line,
Monday, report
that it's hidden
in clouds, out
of mind, until,
in a sudden
wind and vanishing
fog, they look up:
not to worship
but, more, from habit;
the way, once left
home when their men
went to rivet
the thing, they said
morning prayers.
Even on Sunday,
now, of course,
they accept how
the shadow swings
down, leaning
in and away
in elliptic rings
like a sundial.
Or so a high
state official
told them it did,
when they, craning
that broken sky,
sat assembled

there for the long
dedication:
it resembled,
he said, nothing
so much; and laughing
then, said if you
knew where you were
(they laughed too),
and perhaps how far
from the solstice,
you could almost tell
what time it was,
by when the shadow
fell on your house.
Not that the tower
itself would fall,
ever, on such
a quiet meadow
of homes, nor would
the isogonic reaction
affect, even touch,
their elm trees;
the theta conductors
were shielded, at
his personal direction,
he said, so not
to entail any risk
for them, or their families.
A man, then, stood
tall, as if to ask
a first question, but
near him a guard
preserved order.
There was, the speaker
admitted, an odor
caused by the breaker
circuits, but this
was the new power,
in essence, and, as
designed, wouldn't last.
A solar device,

he called it, strong
as the Nation
itself, which, because
of such structures,
would stand until
Kingdom Come.
They were proud there,
then; and still are,
when their children,
or children's children,
home from municipal
lectures, recite,
without prompting,
the smallest detail:
the interval
of each warning light,
and how, just
at dawn, the strange
orange glow
on top will go
out, with something
suspended, like
lazing snow
in the morning air;
not much, a flake
here, a flake there,
which dissolves
to a kind of dust
that settles, daily,
around the globular
base. And, daily,
the child who puts up
the flag is assigned,
also, to sweep.
Once every year
they make wreaths
(of jagged cut felt,
shaped like elm leaves)
and lay them here,
between the new sidewalk
and Main Street.

Otherwise, nothing
is changed: home
is the same, talk
still revolves
around the same
people. Government
studies, given
every control,
have proven
this. The report
is unanimous,
to every intent:
there's been neither
famine nor war.
Their original
fear of the fall
is gone, the range
of the shadow
seems less, the weather
more clear. The meadows
are full of new flowers;
stakes are aligned
on most lawns, shaped
like sundials.
Women count hours
still; they repeat
household trials,
and gossip. But
except for
the fool who tried
climbing the tower,
few have died;
most have escaped
the usual town
diseases; misbegotten
children are
fewer, the suicide
rate is down.
Indeed, nothing
is ominous
here, unless

you take stock
of their dreams:
waking, sometimes,
they say, it hangs
over them: not
exactly the tower
itself, but what
they've forgotten,
something above
the tower, like
a dance tune
they can't quite
remember, or name.
They are used to
the circuit breakers
now; they admit
it, even to
government
census-takers,
who wake them—
women weeping
over their sleeping
men, at dawn—
since only then,
before day
begins, will they
try to show,
without words,
but pointing towards
the tower, that what
they can't name
is, like waking
itself, or making
love, not different,
no, but in spite
of the Government,
yes, not quite
the same.

THE TOTAL CALM

We had, at midnight, flicked the outside light
and watched the first thin spit of snow, a flurried
swirl, as if off some cold edge of heaven
blown with such high force that—where we looked
to see our still bare driveway through the glass,
through floodlit gusts—it seemed the house was driven.

Then in a softened wind, we saw the flat
flakes hang, drift up and spin, until we heard
a squall hiss through the oak's stiff leaves, and guessed
that it had settled down to snow. House locked,
we looked out at the last thin spears of grass
bent through the storm whose forecast we had missed.

Before we banked the fire, the lights went out
the way the stars had gone at dusk. With power
lost, we slept downstairs and, waking cold
beside cold ashes, wondered how we'd weathered
sleep to this faint dawn and yet not heard
some rusted town-plow buck the drifted world.

Mute as birds, we faced a flat gray light:
the snow built up against our plate-glass door
like glacial strata, white on white, as if
some soft slow-motion avalanche had gathered
weight behind it, while we slept, and had
at last been loosened from an unknown cliff.

Into the solstice, then, we woke toward silence;
and listening out in hope some winter bird
might sing, we climbed up-attic where the stretch
of snow—a nowhere left to tunnel to, impassable
tough mounds that might be trees, the earth at zero—
lay blanked as far as our two minds could reach.

It might have, at the year's uneasy balance,
melted out and been the other flood;

yet this ungodly cold, these depths that whelm us,
are let down from altitudes impossible
to judge, as if from emptied realms where snow,
unmelting snow, is all that's left to calm us.

THE OWL

I thought he'd gone, that owl,
to wherever owls winter at.
But no, he's out there still,
hooing the cold, awake
to what small things an owl
can hear under those big fake
horns. My eyes blink shut,
but his are full of the dark,
and see. I saw him once,
at noon, when they wouldn't work,
and he sat sleeping, up
in a deadwood oak, looking more
like a displaced giant moth
than a bird of prey. Except
for his triple talons, which tore
at the branch, or at dreams, while he slept,
he sat unruffled, and aloof.
I tried to stone him off,
but I missed; his dreams were remote,
and swaying, he never woke.
Or say he waited me out.
That was ten days ago,
and I'm still unsure of us both.
By our different lights, we're blind
two ways to our different stake
in these woods. I hear him hoo,
again, and think of the beak
those dove sounds issue from.
I'm frozen, too. I'd sleep
if I could, while he hunts,
but I've got a mind to outlast him.
And this time, but not to cast
stones, I stretch and walk out,
to find what he's hunting for.
Not that I think this first snow
will be full of tracks to identify;
that owl, from whatever tree

he looks down, has only an eye
for what's warm, and shivering
still, with a need to run free.
Awake where my eyes adjust
to the dark, I stand frozen now,
and I begin to see.

THE LINE

It's not, at sea, like crossing the equator,
not a line you're schooled to navigate—
though fools have run their easting down, Capetown
to Perth, solo, in hope old Neptune
would meet them halfway, with a mermaid,
rum, and some engraved certificate.

The initiation is secret, as Conrad knew.
Crossing at night in the Gulf of Siam,
a man can find himself in stays, unsure
of his first command; yet need no braid,
then or again, to weather whatever mutiny.
Nansen froze his way across, in the *Fram.*

Shackleton crossed in the Scotia Sea,
but he, like Captain Slocum, left no chart
to fix the latitude of his crossing. You
could track the *Spray,* sister her hull,
tack to survive Magellan's straits, and still
not cross. It's not a line you'd know to plot

though you signed Bowditch as your navigator.
Until you find yourself hove-down, lost,
in masthead seas, and sight it dead abeam,
no other voyage helps define
your bearing on this course; but once you leave it
clear astern, you'll know what you have crossed.

NIGHT NOTES ON AN OLD DREAM

Like a seal
in broken sleep,
aware of how
cold the moonlight
lies on salt ice,
I let the sea
work. The floodtide
under my skull,
lugged by the full
March moon, under-
cuts the barrier
shelf, folds back, and
opens a lead
to my forehead.
The moon waves in.
Adrift, and washed
by the equinox,
I let the sea
work. Under me
the shelf calves off;
my sleep ebbs East,
offshore. Sure, for
once, I'm neither
mad nor dead, I
dive awake from
the floe where last
night's snowbirds rise;
and I count them,
white and moonstruck,
climbing, beyond
Orion, to the moon
behind my eyes.

SEA-CHANGE

John Marin
(1870–1953)

Marin
saw how it feels:
the first raw shock
of Labrador current,
the surfacing gasp
at jut of rock,
bent sails, and wedged
trees. He wrote it:
Stonington, Small
Point, and Cape Split,
through a pane so
cracked by the lode-
star sun that he
swam back, blinded,
into himself to
sign the after-
image: initialed
mountains, ledged
towns (white as
Machias after
the hayrake rain),
sun-splintered
water and written
granite; dark light
unlike what you
ever saw until,
inland, your own
eyes close and, out
of that sea-change,
islands rise thick:
like the rip-tide
paint that, flooding,
tugs at your vitals,
and is more Maine
than Maine.

MAINE

When old cars get retired they go to Maine.
Thick as cows in backlots off the blacktop,
East of Bucksport, down the washboard
From Penobscot to Castine,
they graze behind frame barns: a Ford
turned tractor, Hudsons chopped to half-ton
trucks, and Chevy panels, jacked up,
tireless, geared to saw a cord of wood.

Old engines never die. Not in Maine,
where men grind valves the way their wives grind axes.
Ring-jobs burned out down the Turnpike
still make revolutions, turned marine.
If Hardscrabble Hill makes her knock,
Maine rigs the water-jacket salt: a man
can fish forever on converted sixes,
and for his mooring sink a V-8 block.

When fishing's poor, a man traps what he can.
Even when a one-horse hearse from Bangor fades
away, the body still survives:
painted lobster, baited—off Route 1—
with home preserves and Indian knives,
she'll net a parlor-full of Fords and haul in
transient Cadillacs like crabs. Maine trades
in staying power, not shiftless drives.

PROPELLER

Caged lightly by two-by-fours, rigged flat
on a low-bed trailer, a bronze propeller
sits stranded off Route 1. It almost
fills both lanes: traffic stacks up
behind it; and each car, passing, reflects
its moment of the five blades' pure color.

Honking won't move such a roadblock.
Halfway, here, from its molten state,
far inland, it waits an ocean: still
to be keyed, then swung home, in a river dredged
with old histories of launching and salvage.
Incomplete though it is, and late,

it will get there, somehow. Even
as a huge tourist attraction, it cost
too much to leave as part of civilization's
roadside debris. It's curious, here,
wondering at the magnitude of such work,
to think how finally diminished

the size will seem, in place, and of how
submerged its ultimate function will be.
But even now, as if geared to a far interior
impulse, it churns the flat light: as far
from here its cast will turn against time,
and turn dark, and it will move the sea.

JAKE'S WHARF

Days like this, off Jake's, the August fog
scales up on millpond mornings. Harbor gulls
float quiet as classboats in the leaning tide
(a gray gull rides the spar buoy on one leg
at noon); by four, blown home, they stand parade
on Jake's streaked roof, and summer moors as Sou'west
smoke furls in across the Camden Hills.

Come Labor Day, these weather-breeders end:
Jake's brightwork dinghies hauled, the mackerel sky
floods schools of rainsqualls on the wharf; September
tides wash through the boatshed where the wind
backs in Northeast; three driven days the timber
creaks, no boat puts off, and only the fish hawks,
cast from bent fir, fish down the spume-lined Bay.

There is another weather then, a day
swung hard Northwest, when every island spruce
stands sharpened in the wind's cold lens and rises,
like Blue Hill, in arctic clarity;
now lobstermen set traps where each wave blazes
in the splintered sun; upriver, seals
lie ledged across the tidal Bagaduce.

Days after these ebb gray without a thaw.
For some few men the winter sea is farmland
and front yard: off Jake's they drag for scallops,
hand-line cod, and tie up cold where tar
and marlin flavor talk that mends the traps.
Time closes in, like snow on cradled yachts,
now people from away have driven inland.

These are the weathers Jake knew to weather out
and wait for, slow in the woodstove warmth of his shop
where, days like this, he used to steam-bend oak,
or bend to plank a skiff, with his weather eye out
for a high March sky. But now, to a snow-swirl wake
of gulls, his lobsterboat swings cold at the mooring;
the wharf leans seaward in the ebb-tide chop.

THE ISLANDERS

Winters when we set our traps offshore
we saw an island farther out than ours,
miraged in midday haze, but lifting clear
at dawn, or late flat light, in cliffs that might
have been sheer ice. It seemed, then, so near,

that each man, turning home with his slim catch,
made promises beyond the limits of his gear
and boat. But mornings we cast off to watch
the memory blur as we attempted it,
and set and hauled on ledges we could fetch

and still come home. Summers, when we washed
inshore again, not one of us would say
the island's name, though none at anchor sloshed
the gurry from his deck without one eye
on that magnetic course the ospreys fished.

Winters, then, we knew which way to steer
beyond marked charts, and saw the island as
first islanders first saw it: who watched it blur
at noon, yet harbored knowing it was real;
and fished, like us, offshore, as if it were.

SABLE ISLAND

60° W—43°56'N

You wouldn't want to go there. Sand
is all there is: a graveyard strip
of ships' bones in the North Atlantic;

backbones, deadeyes, ribs, cast up
like the dune itself, by an antic
surf. Cabot chose not to land.

A Portuguese pilot first named it
Santa Cruz, drifting for fish
on the king's orders; it was longer

then, before the unchristly wash
of wind broke up the bar in stranger
shapes than the Cross, which never formed it.

All known charts, by 1546,
marked its luck as Sable, prized
as bad luck for the centuries

of full-sail trade which civilized
that beach, with skeletons and crosstrees.
Two hundred and fifty known wrecks

ghost it now: Gloucestermen,
British men-o'-war, and Greeks,
Nova Scotiamen, and Vikings.

Henry stranded his Bastille convicts
there, with pardons. A woman with rings
on her fingers, lost there when

the ship *Amelia* sank, with all hands,
had an emerald hacked off her corpse,
by professional wreckers. People have tried

to live there, all right: lighted hopes,
seed, cattle, most of which died.
Ganged horses still churn those sands,

wild as the madmen shipped to asylum,
and burial, there. A Boston parson
petitioned to own it once; but, granted

his gift, could find no sane person
to harvest the crop he claimed his stunted
bushes grew, in that private Elysium.

There was a harbor there, years ago.
But where, only God knows, now that
the tides have sanded it, smooth as an eel.

Save for the cumulus hung in mounted
thermals over those flat dunes, still
as fast-ice, you wouldn't know

a landfall was in the offing; not even
close in, if you'd drifted forty hours
in a lifeboat, and woke with the sea making up,

and the first fog lifted. No upraised oars
will get you help here, half swamped by the chop,
and not so much bound to any haven

ahead as running, hull-down in the heavy
troughs, from any last watch kept aloft,
and all false havens astern. Only the loud

surf sounds this shore, patrolled by a raft
of gulls, and buoyed by the anvil cloud.
Half-drowned fishermen, home from Davy

Jones' fleet, tell how the first boy born
to castaways here will be island king.
But no one yet has survived this beachhead

by divine right, or weathered the breaking
tons of sea to couple his hope with dead
myths. The cloud itself might warn

you away. Yet sighting it first from an open
boat, like many who risk the sea,
you have no choice of refuge left.

You might even, tugged in under the lee
of this island, think yourself safe,
and forget its history, or how you happen

to be here. Seen from a mast-step broken
by gales, it looks huge. As it is. No
matter what new disasters to come, you must shape

your course into the breakers as though
it were the whole world, not just a strip
of blown sand you happen to be cast up on.

III.

HEART OF DARKNESS

*You ought to have heard him recite
poetry, his own, too, it was . . . Oh,
he enlarged my mind.*
                    —The Harlequin Seaman

Exterminate the brutes.
We remember that part.
We remember Kurtz,
and his final horror.
To say he only pretended
to be of the new gang,
the gang of virtue,
is not to have read
the full Report.
Or is not to have been there.
Marlow, of course, knew.
He was there. But recall
how he had to lie,
as a matter of conscience,
to get himself back.
We know that. We, too,
have rivets and work,
science, and new
editions of *Towson's
Inquiry* to occupy
our minds. Efficiency
is what saves us.
It would be an error,
though, to imagine
that Marlow's tale
was ever conclusive.
As they knew on the *Nellie,*
counting a river
of flickering lights,
and waiting out a night
tide, there's not much
to go on: The Intended,
with her blindfold and torch,
the background near black;

and always in a white suit,
the Chief Accountant;
chained natives, dying;
popguns firing into
a continent's underbelly,
a few shrunken heads
on some pointed sticks;
and, yes, the voice—
vox clamantis—we know
all that. But the center,
the center is still elusive.
We must find the poem.
One that, again, might
enlarge our harlequin
mind. Lost as we
are, with no choice
of nightmares left,
but only stakes
higher than Kurtz
could dream of, what
we need is the poem.
Not that we'll ever
get back to where we,
in our virtue, began.
But if, at least,
we try for some coastal
station, the poem,
the poem that must
map the bottom
of here, would be
some sort of base
to start out from.

THAT CLEAR FIRST MORNING

That clear first morning after,
maybe turned sixteen, I
first stayed up all night

and woke from waking
to see the sun break open,
happening to the simple world:

there were people there,
who slept while I was waking,
and were waking while I woke.

I was where they were.
There were men waking to coffee
and lunch boxes, women

tending the coffee and making
lunches. They were me.
I was there, being young.

Whoever it was I'd waited up
to meet kept coming around
the corner I kept turning,

certain and new as the sun.
Beginning with that sure morning,
I slept in having begun.

THE DAY THE TIDE

The day the tide went out,
and stayed, not just at Mean
Low Water or Spring Ebb,
but out, out all the way
perhaps as far as Spain,
until the bay was empty,

it left us looking down
at what the sea, and our
reflections on it, had
(for generations of
good fish, and wives fair
as vessels) saved us from.

We watched our fishboats ground
themselves, limp-chained in mud;
careened, as we still are
(though they lie far below us)
against this sudden slope
that once looked like a harbor.

We're level, still, with islands,
or what's still left of them
now that treelines invert:
the basin foothills rock
into view like defeated castles,
with green and a flagpole on top.

Awkward as faith itself,
heron still stand on one leg
in trenches the old tide cut;
maybe they know what the moon's
about, working its gravity
off the Atlantic shelf.

Blind as starfish, we
look into our dried reservoir

of disaster: fouled trawls, old
ships hung up on their mon-
ument ribs; the skeletons
of which our fathers were master.

We salt such bones down with self-
consolation, left to survive,
if we will, on this emptied slope.
Réunion Radio keeps reporting
how our ebb finally flooded
the terrible Cape of Good Hope.

DENYING THE DAY'S MILE

Always on clear mornings
I wake across their valley
to face the day's horizon:
quickened by my tentative
steps, I leap it like
the solo shadow of a big
jet—behind which I
am the sun.
                By the time
dusk takes my neighbor's
streetcorner, and staggers
me home, I'm overcast
always: I imagine men
in the Andaman Islands
waking to fish, women
giving breast in Lhasa
to children the color of rice.
But I can never conceive
what weather they wake to, or
face those multiple hands
that bait my eye to a map.
I've never even been sure
whether they're still beginning
a day I've already lost,
or a day I haven't begun.
Even with my ear close
as a child's to waves
bounced off Afghanistan,
the Black Sea, and London,
there is too much static
to pick up children eating
fists of Tibetan snow.
Before God died, I thought
it might be fun to try
his game for a while: not
to judge the world, but simply
to listen in on how

it was getting on. Now
I couldn't bear it: I can't
even stand my neighbors,
or face myself when I go
to bed with no love left
from the day.
                Always on clear
mornings I wake intending
to walk a mile, and to hold
that mile's particulars up
to the general flight of jets,
as they pretend to climb
over human weather, and land
on cement deserts that have
nothing to do with love.
I am overcast always
for having flown to escape
wild chicory I might
have picked for my wife, the man
next door I hate, and this
lousy city that managed,
without God, to smog itself
through another November day.
If I were pilot tomorrow,
I'd fly for better weather;
but tonight I'm not even
myself: where I haven't been
is already yesterday.

VOYAGES

Crouched hard on granite,
facing a weathered sea,
I breathe as slow as rock.

Harbor is one way to look;
but voyages wash my eye,
and old tides rock my butt.

Gulls root on the ledge,
taught by every wind
how spruces tug; snails

hug the tideline, hulls
on their own horizon: bound
as I am to the very edge.

OFFSHORE

The bay was anchor, sky
and island: a land's end
sail, and the world tidal,
that day of blue and boat.

The island swam in the wind
all noon, a seal until
the sun furled down. Orion
loomed, that night, from unfathomed

tides; the flooding sky
was Baltic with thick stars.
On watch for whatever catch,
we coursed that open sea

as if by stars sailed off
the chart; we crewed with Arc-
turus, Vega, Polaris,
tacking into the dark.

SEAWEED

Ontogeny recapitulates phylogeny

Naked on island rock,
bodied with salt in the late
sun, we dry and look down:
golden wilds of seaweed
garden the dive we surfaced from.

Stripped to who we once were,
we submerged in the wash
of floodtide: man and bride,
we swam who we might become.
After the ebb taught us love

we climbed out of the sea;
but if there are seaweed gods
I think we are wed by them:
I feel salt still on your back,
your bones swim under me.

TENANTS HARBOR

Listen, the tide has turned:
you can hear yesterday's left-
over swell, fooling around

against Condon's Rock. Who's
to care where the cold front went,
when it lifted a week of nimbus

clear of the Camden Hills?
Somebody's probably mapped it,
as part of a spiral,

current from Canso
to Gander; people are always
pulsing their plot of distance

from storms, from a weapons-system,
a star, or a war. Safe
from radar, we're eased home

by how the wind climbed out
of the cove, and leaned Orion
down to this summer's last night.

Tomorrow, counting our change
at a tollgate, we'll suck
on a hot inland orange

for lunch, gas up to anchor
ourselves to a map, and plot
the cost of a winter ashore.

Tonight we only chart
ourselves, in how through spruce
the thick stars constellate;

this side of Condon's Rock
we're tenant to two black ducks,
discussing themselves in the dark.

Who's to tell them the world
lies elsewhere? Not you,
nor I, who migrate. The world

is wherever we quiet to hear it.
Tides darken our listening;
comic as ducks, we share it.

CIDER

Downhill through this upland meadow,
    aster and chicory, sumac,
    poplar and apple,
distill into Fall: its cider light
opens the deepening woods, de-
    canting, through leaves, this
    stillness a hundred feet tall.

Secret in their seasonal shadow,
    chipmunk quip, the tick
    of felled acorns, thick bees,
speak only their season's self-praise.
There is no password or resident
    God; only this upland light,
    fallen through miles of trees.

DEER ISLE

Out-island once, on a South slope
bare in March, I saw a buck
limp out of the spruce and snow
to ease his gut in a hummocky meadow.

He fed two rooted hours on the hope
of spring, browsed, and flicked back
into the trees, a big ghost
of what hunters tracked at first frost.

That was six winters ago. Today,
three hundred miles South, a commuter
trapped by a detour sign
at dusk, I trailed a reflecting line

of red arrows that took me the long way
home. Late, caught in the neuter
traffic, driven beyond where I wanted
to go, I braked by a slanted

orchard where six cars were stopped.
There were six does there, feeding on frozen
winesaps, fat and white-rumped
as the drivers who sat in their cars. One limped,

and I thought of that buck, equipped
to survive, on the island he'd chosen
to swim to. That coast, about now,
would lie gray: the raw salt snow

topping a man's hauled lobsterpots,
and sifting down through thick spruce
where the sweat on a run buck
would freeze. A man with no luck

but a gun would be hunting home cross-lots.
I was parked miles beyond choice,
miles from home on a blocked curve
in the dead midst of a thick suburban preserve.

My guts clamped. I honked my way clear,
tramping the gas toward nowhere
but where home was. My wife understood.
If I didn't go now I never would.

A REFUSAL OF STILL PERFECTIONS

That bare farm stripped of summer
drifts in my sleep. The river below
its field is salt, tidal, and blue.
I own how that farm rests white
on white: barn on house on snow.

But I know I can never live there.
Never, for pasture, mortgage the river,
or pawn dark hopes to insure old sleep.
The fence behind me casts tidal shadows.
I wake to mornings I'd better keep.

REFUSING THE SEA

I

As headlands weather a gale,
and barns sleep against weather,
the sea argues hemlock and rock.

Granite and dwarf-pine fend
against wind; the moon floods in
where the ebb tries to tack.

Tonight is nobody's harbor.
Make-and-break fishermen tide
themselves over: they lock

their nets on the groundswell bottom,
and plow offshore to ride
the night out. Their gunwales wash black

and roll clear: the helmsman's eye
is decked with moons. But everyman
fished in his forepeak hammock

sleeps like a gimbaled compass.
As herring survive who school
beyond coves and harbor wrack,

men slept hove-to over fifty
fathoms will, silvered by
fish-scales, net coming back.

II

The bellbuoy rang its tides
all night, banging its changes
against sleep's undertow.

At night in Maine, all night,
the wind climbs into the elms;
the stars revolve their slow

old pattern, turning the moon
to lure new schools of herring.
And we, on Main Street, bloated

with heirloom rum, choke
on our fishbone nightmares: son
like father, we never boated

a fish, or gambled a widow
to cast for ourselves. We bank
in Boston, refusing the sea,

while men with Mediterranean
names gaff our daughters
to bed. Porpoises sport

the morning tide while we
tend shop on a chamber pot,
and settle our will in chancery.

AFTER THE *THRESHER*

sunk with all hands off the
Atlantic shelf, April 10, 1963

There must be people, if
there are still people, who
somewhere yet above us

(where there are even birds)
breathe, swim, and survive
at their bright apogee

while we, under pressure,
gasp, weigh on each other,
and collapse face to face.

Even this sea-level smog
would seem like graced light
to signalmen tapping out code

from a locked hull, sounding
their own slow taps from the coast's
dark beer-can floor.

Trying to face them, we stretch
to imagine release, fail
to imagine ourselves, and try

to decompress with another
iced drink: the lawnspray squeaks,
and traffic begins to thunder

as if it were Sunday somewhere.
But we have been sunk for months,
under tons of possible air.

NTHIA'S WEATHERS

in memory of Cynthia Pyle
(1924–1965)

Listen, you winds,
receive her gently.

And you, you weathers,
accept her own.

She felt them quickly:
winds backed East

on a falling glass,
and gray old pressures

of tide, ebbing
against the sun.

Afraid of islands,
she loved this harbor;

a mother shored up
by now, from the wharf,

she watched a daughter
raise sail and cast off,

racing herself
to make a late start.

Gentle her, winds.
And you, you offshore

weathers, take her
to heart: tide her over

who loved this harbor.
Even here, she hurt.

CLEANING OUT THE GARAGE

for J. B. F.

Hooks, screw-eyes, and screws; the walls
thick with bent nails to catch on: somebody's
grandfather must have hoped his grandson
would use these nicked tools. Adze, spoke-shave,
and saw hang with dead moth-wings, spidered
to leaning studs. Fifty winters have heaved
this catch-all off its foundations, cracked
the poured-floor, and left to mildew the tent
I almost slept in, moored to my boyhood backyard.

Sponges that bilged three lapstrake rowboats
(the lot of them rotted or sunk) stiffen
like pockmarked soft footballs; instructions
for washing the Model-T Ford curl tacked
to the faucet plank. The wall is shelved
with paintcans left to weather, their paint
skinned like my grandfather's wrinkles. The gloss
has gone soft on his set of golf clubs: troon,
nap-iron, and niblick, bagged with balls but no
putter, their hickory shafts still true.

It's summer when I haul back to all this:
a goldfinch dead in a box of unplanted
seeds, chemicals bagged to poison the weeds
that still flourish. Stormed by the dust
of my sweeping, storm windows lean stacked
like the panes my boyhood couldn't see through.
I try to sweep out the useless stuff I still
cherish: a drugstore sloop that tipped over,
a bathtub submarine that floated between
my legs like a small sick fish; I try not
to sink in this scrap I dive to uncover.

Cars jacked up here, in '18 and '43,
the Ford and a Chevy, still stain the cracked floor
with drip from their oilpans; my great-

grandfather's (substitute's) Civil War sword
points North like the rusted compass my family
never trusted: in all the winters somebody
shoveled a path to this island garage,
there was gear for voyages, wars, or rebuilding;
enough to see whole generations through.
I'm game for different winters in this high summer;
a woman I loved who refused me taught me what I
mean to leave here: how to let go what won't do.

FORECAST

The late fog, lifting.
A first wind, risen.
The long tide, at ebb.

And cast off finally,
into that routine hope,
the fishboats: going out.

THE SHIP

Watches North of the tropics,
still dwarfed by the ocean that pocked
her iron plates, she's anchored herself

off Searsport; and swung on her hook
for a week's end, a salt-mile offshore.
Searsport's no liberty port;

it's barely a harbor: a wharf,
a tidal point of white houses,
thick with their cargo of snow.

Nobody local knows why
she's here, her fires apparently
banked, with only the rusted

top of her smokestack smudging
the frozen air. Talk says
that her crew's all sick, but men

on a catwalk bend to chip paint;
others stand watch on the wings
of her bridge in what, through binoc-

ulars, looks like health.
She's flown no quarantine flag;
no boat's put ashore for a doctor,

water, or food. Nobody's
even landed, in fact, to pay
some small respect to the Harbor-

master. Because of the rumor
of plague, he's ordered the fishboats
to stay in port. The windows

of every drowned grandfather's house
are busy with rumor's widows:
not so much watching the ship

herself as watching their husbands
congress the wharf. They all
agree, by her Plimsoll marks,

that she's slightly down by the bow,
perhaps because of the crates
on her foredeck. Still, she's shown

no sign of distress; although
her sheer is foreign, her lights
conform to International

Rules: the consensus is
that she isn't Russian. But no man
wakes in Searsport who doesn't

get up to look for her flag;
the women, had they a right word,
would pray some name on her transom.

If only she'd signal her business,
call *M'aidez!* or put in for help,
Searsport might ease its distress.

Searsport's sent more captains
to sea than any Maine port
in history; its children, even,

are baptized by disaster.
Yet even the town's most famous
son, a mutineer hung

in the crosstrees, could never
imagine an old tramp tired
of passage, who simply put in

in need of reflection at anchor.
Whatever port Searsport once was,
she found it no harbor-of-refuge;

after she'd lain here only
three days, and kept her own
silence from Friday through Sunday,

every white house and upright
church, self-exiled by anger,
prided itself with outrage.

Whatever her registry, tonnage,
or name, whatever it was
she came for, Searsport delivered

no goods to her hold and recovered
no profit from what she might light.
She stoked up her fires early

this morning, and weighed her great hook
before breakfast. Watching
her hull, and then her thin plume

of smoke, sink over the known
horizon, the town stood as close
to attention as Maine is ever,

with strangers, likely to get.
As long as men fish, her wake's
bound to roil the turned tide,

and churn the fogged bell
the fishboats bear on, sounding
their own thin horns to locate

each other. Until Searsport
melts, or the Bay freezes over,
the natives are liable to never

recover: denying this coast
as if it didn't exist,
the ship made raw her departure

around the Three Mile black buoy.
It's always been out there, seaward
of every quilt bed and the town's

five steeples: a secular bell
for the exiled ear to home on,
tended by gulls in its floating

cage, tolling both warning
and sea-room. Nobody paid it
much mind until this morning:

the ship, edging out, gave it
nine great blasts on her horn,
as if in familiar salute.

IV.

SUPPOSITION WITH QUALIFICATION

If he could say it, he meant to.
Not what it meant, if he ever knew,

but how it felt when he let himself
feel—even afraid of himself—

yet in that moment opened
himself to how the moment happened.

He meant to give himself up:
to how it could be when he gave up

requiring that each event shape
itself to his shape, his hope,

and intent. He meant not to weigh it,
whatever happened; only to let it

balance in its own light, to let light
fall where it would. If he could say it.

THE MAN ON THE WHARF

The man on the wharf, watching a man
shuck clams on the wharf, stands into

the wind as if he hung on a mooring.
Rolling drunk, his sea-legs are stable;

he watches the boats go out and come in.
He casts off himself when they sail;

when they harbor they harbor toward him.
Wherever they sail or haul herring,

the man on the wharf has already been.
His fogged eye telescopes ports,

and multiplies one clear woman.
Her breasts were islands to home on,

sea-marks off his home cove, until
last winter sank her. Skim-ice ate

at the wharf through March. Like cancer.
Or like a surgeon cutting through it.

The man on the wharf cannot remember
which. Or why he stands into the wind,

watching a man shuck clams on the wharf,
watching as if his hand held the knife.

He watches himself watching, in mind
of his son who will not write him, cut

by the wind that quicks through his workshirt,
by sunlight glinting the waves like knives.

He pisses behind the boatshed, warm
where his body performs its remaining function;

then sucks at his pint of Jim Beam, relieved.
Rolled back into the wind again,

he watches the man shuck clams on the wharf.
He's almost calm, who swallows no answer,

but questions in bourbon this seeming harbor,
this harbor where he has always lived.

Distilled by October sun, its hill-
sides bourbon, its trees thinned to rust,

it leaves him no choice of winters, no
skipper whose last command he might balk at,

now that the fishboats have cast him off.
They harbor downwind, rolling drunkenly

toward him.
              The sea is all he can ask.

THE QUESTION POEM

It can never be satisfied, the mind, never.
—Wallace Stevens

I

What does it mean, the wind?
And that thick, concurrent, shift
of wings, flighted to swim
this dune: what tidal will,
if will there is, schools these
quick sanderlings to print
their hundred feet a half-
mile down the beach?
              Who knows
what sudden discipline
decides their strict migration?

II

What asks a man, on the tide's
hard sand, to fly his words
into the wind, with or beyond
the shorebirds?
              Who's to say
if the snowy egret, judging
the ebb from her solo leg,
poised in a tidal pool,
fishes to answer more
than her own stiff gut?
              And what
high knowledge cools the osprey,
risen offshore on this hot dune's
thermals, stooping his shadow
across cold navies of herring?

III

The whole Cape tips as the sun
climbs; a half-mile short

of flight, my toes curl in
toward clamflat questions, questions
that the tide's grave music
rises to inhabit: may not
the universe expand
by what life asks of it?
Or does the farthest edge
contract if man, grown tense
on his small margin, fits
an empty limpet shell
to his soft impotence?
The sanderlings lift, forming
divergent nebulae,
tipped edgewise into the sky's
great ocean; the wind's plankton,
the sun's birds, the sea
and dune own shape and motion:
what matter to them, or me,
if cells divide to multi-
ply, or atoms constellate,
with more or less intention?

IV

Presumptive, still, among
the sea's fugitive creatures,
who am I to wade out into
the sea's unwritten poem?
Why should I care if the sea
is careless?
              Submerged in the wind
without wing or fin, a man
only fit to bargain with women,
I cannot imagine the world
without me; I wait to meet
the blind moon's tide, asking
the sea what I myself mean,
and if I mean what I ask:

can there be any question?

THE STRANDING

When I put my eyes up to
the eyes of my skull and
look in through both eyes

at once, out beyond shoals
of porpoises that sport
as if they'd been whelped in

my inner ear, all I can see
is myself at infinite
focus: a man the tide caught

on that same tidal ledge
where all his life
he has gathered kelp.

I can barely make out
his blue jacket and seaboots.
The tide is still coming.

His skiff is already gone.
It's already gotten dark
at the top of my skull;

through cracks in that sky
the Northern birds are homing.
Wreaths of kelp float up

through the bedrock; if I
weren't stranded so far
from myself, or if

the wind veered, I might try
to yell his name. But he's
already begun to listen

to how, as they whistle
and roll to breathe,
the porpoises click for sea room.

THANKSGIVING

The tides in my eye are heavy.
My grandmother's house wears oakleaves
instead of nasturtiums; hollyhocks
dry in the front-porch gutter.
I must have been a bad boy,
exiled under the attic stairs:
a hardwood hatrack plants
its Black-Eyed petals under my nose,
but I have no hat to top it.
I reach, instead, to touch the face
of the harvest moon, full on the face
of my mother's grandfather's clock.
My fingers tick, but the clock
will not relent; I cannot wind
nor strike it.
                    I only smell
the locked closets, the open shelves
of jarred preserves that grow
their quiet mold in the old back pantry.
My ears are mice, peaked to the sizzle
of badly bottled homemade rootbeer.
It was once Thanksgiving all week.
And we ate all day from the five pies
baked in the coalstove oven—after
the peas put up from summer, and squash
put down in the cellar. I cannot say
what else lies under my tongue.
My mother's mouth is grave with snow;
on the hill where she, too, was once young.

HARD COUNTRY

In hard
country each white
house, separated
by granite outcrop
from each white
house, pitches
its roofline
against the hard sky.
Hand-split
shakes, fillet
and face plank, clap-
board, flashing
and lintel: every
fit part over-
laps from the ridge
board on down, wind-
tight and water-
tight, down
to the sideyard back
door, shut against
eavesdrop.

Nobody
takes storm windows
off: each blank
pane, framed by
its own sharp
molding, looks out
without shutters at
juniper, granite,
and hackmatack.
Granite takes
nothing for granted,
hackmatack's spiny;
junipers mind their
ledged roots. Save
for a day when its back

door opens on lilac,
there isn't a house
in this country
that sleeps or
wakes.

In hard
country Orion,
come summer, hunts
late; but belts its
prime stars all
winter when sun
is short: each white
house, separated
by granite outcrop
from each white
house, pitches
its private roof
against horizon
and season; each white
clapboard, wind-
tight and water-
tight, juts
against weather
its own four inches
of shadow and
light.

THE GATE

Retreated from supper
into the pasture, he
steps himself up to

the rock his horses statue,
watching the sun let go
milkweed and aster. He

thinks the whole world
is going to seed. Fingering
burdock, at odds with horses,

asters and women, he
poses himself against
the long sunset. The season

sinks: its last light
shadows the rock he stands on.
Not light, but shadows,

lift from limestone
the fossils that centuries
press at his feet: backbone

and ribcage pressed out
of this outcrop! Fish,
for Christ's sake! The imprint

of fins! His feet light
as fishbones, walking down
lakes the horses swam out of,

he sprints back through aster
and milkweed, homing into
the nuzzle of horses: mare

and stallion looking for oats.
They follow him, up to the gate.
He floats home, under

the light of dead stars, returned
from this field's large history
into the world of small wars.

POEMS

Not dead elms fallen, but
greenwood blazed by choice,

felled, and then lugged out
in lengths a man can shoulder.

The heartwood wet, the log raw
with its weight of sap; the man

who slashed at branches lugs it,
hefting its length to fit

his sawhorse: he bucks it out,
sweating his tail off, under

the low shed roof of a cold
November sky. His saw jams,

on knots that once gave leaves
to an April wind. His own limbs

ache, stiff with birthdays;
his wife kisses him, proud of

labor, generous with Sunday beer.
She wants to pile level

the wood she leans on to free
for his saw. But he means to stack

his own end-grain. Piece by piece,
counting concentric rings, he figures

not only the warmth of this house
but who may, maybe, differently

love him; love the ease, the sweat grain
and heat, in a house that may not

be his: a man gone early to stranger
work—a morning woman left sweetly

to season, reading the coals
of a slow old hardwood fire.

LINES FROM AN ORCHARD
ONCE SURVEYED BY THOREAU

I've lived by the world's rules
long enough. That season is over.
There's no ladder, no word that the bees
haven't already given. My feet
press cider back to the roots.
The orchard quiets: I sip
at its silence, letting the nectar
change me. What else
need I know, when there's
nothing to know, save
for the wisdom of trees?
I conduct myself like a naked monk.
Were I to open
to any more fullness, I think I'd
turn into a woman.

NATIVE TO VALLEYS

Native to valleys, crossed
by the sun as the sun comes up,
I wake to a mirror of hardwood,

facing myself in the shape
of familiar hills. They tier
to my eye ridge beyond ridge:

each plotted farm a map
of my morning limits, wrinkled
to cowpath and furrow; each

skyline tree and high pasture
horizons of my own nature.
And you, still shadowed by sleep:

I watch you wake in the sharp
relief of descending light,
the fog burned off those rivers

that dreamt you seaward, your ears
happy with trains. Our waking,
far downriver and up,

faces the grain of the land:
a river empty of trestles,
streams and gullies steep

as eroded drumlins. We grope
for clothes and coffee, our selves
woken by waking beside

each other: who climb back down
from separate sleep
and are, by morning, married.

TRIPLE EXPOSURE

I

Secret at heart,
he lugs it out
of sight, pressed

tightly against
himself: not on
his sleeve, but un-

der his coat, sewn
in his left breast
pocket. He shakes

when people meet
him, trying to
fight the closing

walls, hoping they
do not know it.
He knows it won't

wear well, lying
there in hard shape,
up against his

throat, stitched by
double-ought thread
to the shirt pressed

under his Navy
blazer. But that
is where it is.

He tacks across
the room, and back,
in careful fits

and starts, stranger
to himself, trying
not to show it.

II

In flight, always
in flight, he veers
away from the harbor's

high traffic: gulls
white as sails, sails
high as gulls.

Beyond joy or anger,
even on these clear
days, he hangs tensed

by the wind, his hurt
wing spread like his
good wing, still unable

to glide, still not
able to locate
the pain. Swung out

over the Bay, back
over the town, he
dives, climbs: a pendulum

timed to mindless
tides, trying to free
himself from himself.

He anchors his eye
on the fishwharf, as if
he were starved. But what

tugs his eye eats
at his gut: he craves
free air to glide on,

to breathe at the tip
of his wings. He veers
away from it, high as

a bird of prey, the day
clear, the harbor under
him small but perfect.

In magnified flight, again
and again, he hangs himself
on the wind, his hurt

wing spread like his
good wing, the gulls
high as sails, the sails

white as gulls: still un-
able to glide, still not
able to locate the pain.

III

He liked trees better
than people. But never,
in truth, walked the deep

woods. Foot by foot, season
by season, he mapped
the hard coast, pretending

himself a seabird, avoiding
feeders, suet, and birdseed.
He programed himself to walk

barefoot, touching his toes
from stone to boulder, until
his feet ached to freeze.

He rocked all winter, from
cliff to tide around the whole
island, coldly looking to sea:

looking to rescue some one
stranger—who natively spoke
the old language of trees.

CROSSTREES

He'd followed the telephone wires for miles, a wire
on each arm of the poles' tall crosstrees. Now
the ground was level, a kind of plateau.

Save for the poles and their solo wires high
on each crossarm, he'd been for two days above treeline.
The deer were small, their miniature faces facing

away from him as they browsed; they fed back over
the treeless distance he had already come.
Even at noon, the stunted deer sought

no cover; the last fawn he passed, at arm's length,
fed blind on white lichen. He couldn't
recall having climbed: the long horizon

behind him was flat in familiar sun, the marrow
of each hard crossarm sharply wired to
its own hard shadow. For two days now

he had not been afraid; but now, in his third dry dawn,
the sky would not quicken. He felt like a deer
gone blind in that morning's bright haze. But then

it opened: where wires from the nearest crossarm
sagged into infinite sunlight, out into what
might have once been across but was not,

the plateau split to a depth without bottom.
His eyes locked on the gap they met, he grabbed
for the ground with his knees and held on;

his eyes closed down to stretch focus. His wrists
pressed back at the edge, against the steep thrust
of a miniature city: a city so deeply sunk

that its buildings had no foundation, but
lifted clear in their own improbable light.
They were pockmarked with caves, but warm as the wall

in a painting of martyrs. Save for the wires
stretched over him, humming gently, thinned into
nowhere, nothing was filigree here: the beechtree

centered within the city bared its dead limbs
in brilliant cantilever; the sandtraps roofing
each building were perfectly raked, the tines

of each rake turned up and left naked.
He dug his toes into the hard plateau, trying
to trench his way back to known maps or

nameable wars. *Jesus God,* he said, before
the deer nosed toward him, *I once shot a thirty-two
on the back nine at Delft. And now I'm not even*

*myself, with nobody left to tell what I
came to, or how I got here or where it was.* The sun,
when he said these things, was still climbing, and

would not let him let go or draw back to sleep.
Jesus God, he said, when the time came. The mouths
of the deer were soft as the mouths of sheep.

BOLT

It's shot all right: this bolt about
as long as a small boy's forearm, thick
as a man's first finger—except
for its square iron head and square nut,

the female threads frozen by rust
to the bolt itself: gorged and ridged
like a mined-out range of hills,
maybe on some peninsula

far to the North. A cold salt fog
has finally settled its dust. Its pits
are dark as marrow, the oxidized ridges
lifted gold: like ferrous tailings

the sun only recently left. God
only knows what it once held together,
what weathered away or broke up
around it: buckboard or keelson,

furnace or plow; the atmosphere
transported and fired them. Feral, now,
too crude to be more than a primitive
weapon, it's simply itself: a bolt

cast up by tides that can't float it.
With nothing else left, a man kneels
over it carefully, here on a shore
where the stones themselves are adrift.

LABRADOR RIVER

A half-day North of Nain,
on the South bank of the Fraser River,

two men sit hunched in blown snow.
One wears a hat like a red wool mitten.

He's wrapped in fur; the other is hooded in
a hide anorak. Slightly apart,

but married to their decision, a woman
in a white parka waits with them, her back

turned to the river they face. A fourth figure,
nearest the river, is insulated from all

the rest; he might be only
a slumped stone cairn. Three, then,

or four: the wind behind them has blown
stiff clumps of grass bare, and peaked

the hood of the woman's white parka.
The Fraser is frozen solid, its salt ice

waved by sastrugi; on the river's
far bank, beyond stunted conifers,

the smoked horizon is long without sun.
No boat is due this season; they don't

expect the boat. Native, they know
they're halfway to the Pole; they don't need stars

to remind them of that. Nor do they
want maps or charts of this coast;

they have every inlet by heart. Why
or how they got here, nobody's said.

Maybe somebody left a question
hanging; or maybe, this half-day North

of Nain, on the South bank of the Fraser,
there's an answer they've barely got wind of.

The wind in its own right searches their wrists.
Hunched against it, expectantly dressed,

the three (or four) of them hold their meeting.
They are met. They hold. They are waiting.

TO CHEKHOV

in a November when I could bear to
read nobody else

Finally
I have come to you.

Out from behind
hard mountains that looked

like the Urals when I
looked back a last time, back

across the low river,
the old rope-ferry sagging

downstream: I think, now,
of the ferryman weighed

by the army greatcoat
I left him on the far bank.

My gray mare dances sideways
across the shadowless steppe,

spooked by my hatless
shadow. Whenever we reach

the Donetz Station, where you
are already waiting, I have

to tell you how a fat
troika-driver, going the other

way, tipped me his hat,
and why I could not salute back.

And you, I expect, will know
his three geldings by name;

and will tell me the driver's
story, knowing who owns him,

and by what human motive,
on this particular

day, he drove his troika
to mountains beyond the river.

There is much about myself
that I do not believe;

much about the river,
and every mountain behind it,

I cannot yet love.
Yet owing to what you

wrote me, I ride to meet you.
Slowed as I am by how

my mind drifts sideways,
I give my mare free reign,

dancing sideways toward
the Donetz Station: you

will be there, waiting,
to tell me where I've been.

ENTRY

Sheer cold here.
Four straight days
below zero, the roof
contracting in
small explosions
all night. Now snow:
snow halfway up
the back shed;
more coming all
morning: the sky
drifted, patched
blue, flakes in
large sizes
lazing against
a small sun.
Around here
they call
these days "open
and shut," by
sunset the wind
will veer and
stiffen; tomorrow
will build on
a windblown
crust. Given
this day, none
better, I try
these words to
quicken
the silence: I
break track
across it
to make myself
known.

THE WINTER OF THE SEPARATION

Where I grew up everything snowed:
from inches to feet of silence, falling
out of the ceiling, onto my bed.
When I came down with the chicken pox,
the field was mica under the phone wires
out the bathroom window. There was no shadow,
not any morning, save in the depth
of my bootprints. I was snowed in,
season on season, size six-and-a-half
in my ski boots, out under weighted pines
with my pheasant tracks and the rabbit stains.
Mothers didn't have skis in that ice age,
my father was always away, and there
never was wind where I drifted, up
to my waist in igloos. Once, through small snow,
my mother came out in her own new flurry
to call me home: she held out the back
of a black kid glove to let one crystal settle.
She explained, she tried to explain, all sides.
When her hand barely touched me, I melted.

STOVE

I wake up in the bed my grandmother died in.
November rain. The whole house is cold.
Long stairs, two rooms through to the kitchen:
walls that haven't been painted
in sixty years. They must have shone then:
pale sun, new pumpkin, old pine.

Nothing shines now but the nickel trim
on the grandmother stove, an iron invention
the whole room leans to surround; even
when it is dead the dogs sleep close behind it.
Now they bark out, but let rain return them;
they can smell how the stove is going to be lit.

Small chips of pine from the woodshed. Then
hardwood kindling. I build it all into the firebox,
on top of loose wads of last June's *Bangor News.*
Under the grate, my first match
catches. Flames congregate, the dogs watch,
the stove begins to attend old wisdom.

After the first noisy moments, I listen for Lora;
she cooked all the mornings my grandmother died,
she ruled the whole kitchen the year I was seven:
I can see Boyd Varnum, a post outside the side door;
he's waiting for Lora, up in the front of the house,
to get right change for his winter squash. Lora says

Boyd's got the best winter squash in the village.
When Boyd gets paid, she ties her apron back on
and lets in the eggman. He has a green wagon.
Lora tells him how last night her husband hit her;
she shows him the marks. All her bruised arms
adjust dampers and vents; under the plates where turnips

are coming to boil, she shifts both pies in the oven.
The dogs feel warmer now. I bank on thick coal.

The panes steam up as sure as November: rain,
school, a talkative stove to come home to at noon;
and Lora sets my red mittens to dry on the nickel shelves
next to the stovepipe. Lora knitted my mittens.

I can still smell the litter of spaniels
whelped between the stove and the wall; there's
venison cooking, there's milktoast being warmed on
the farthest back plate, milktoast to send upstairs
to my dead mother's mother. Because, Lora says,
she is sick. Lora says she is awful sick. When Lora goes up

to my grandmother's bed, I play with the puppies
under the stove; after they suckle and go back to sleep,
because I am in second grade and am seven, I practice
reading the black iron letters raised on the black oven door;
even though I don't know who Queen Clarion was,
I'm proud I can read what the oven door says: it says

        Queen Clarion
        Wood & Bishop
        Bangor, Maine
        1911

DARK

This is the pure time.

Nobody but me is awake.
Not in this house. Nobody
anywhere that I know.

But everyone I imagine.

A nurse in mid-shift, over coffee,
telling her probie to keep
a good eye on 514.

A hundred miles due north
of this house, a switchman
shoveling freightyard drifts,

his torch waiting for trains.
The gulls on Jake's Wharf,
still folded in sleep, dreaming

as far as gulls dream: of
the new town dump. One Old Squaw,
a black duck with both eyes open,

already woken in the Back Cove.

I've only begun to see how
I feel, to believe who I am,
to trust what I know.

It's time.

Exactly six months from now,
to the moment, the sun will just
have come up through this window.

A LATE SPRING: EASTPORT

On the far side
of the storm
window, as close

as a tree
might grow to
a house,

beads of rain
hang cold
on the lilac:

at the tip of
each twig each
bud swells green;

tonight out
there each
branch will be

glazed, each
drop will
freeze solid:

the ice, at
sunrise, will
magnify every

single
bud; by this
time next

week, in-
side this
old glass,

the whole
room will
bloom.

THE WAY TIDE COMES

It came close from out far,
the way tide comes, changing
its levels with such consistent
slowness that—before I
knew it—height became depth,
and where you danced barefoot,

a half-tide ago, covered itself,
under so moving a shimmer
I could not conceive of the weight,
or recall all those shapes
the weight, as it climbed, erased.
We'd kept to old ways, building

a beachfire well above tideline,
ritual at the pure height of summer;
we'd piled driftwood on,
all we could gather. I was
skipping flat stones, you
were trying to keep count; leaning

to throw, I felt distances shift:
it was no longer coming but
like the light of summer itself,
longest the day when summer began,
had already flooded and made
its insistent turn. As once it came

slowly, so now it pulls back
with the quick of evening light:
it will, in due time, uncover
the farthest rocks we swam up on,
even the morning shallows where we
first waded. Tonight's full moon

has already cast off the horizon
it hugely climbed; it's going, before

long, to tug the whole cove empty.
We slept once pretending a larger
knowledge; now we love better.
Let love be: let the heel-and-toe

of your improvised jig, marginal
even at noon, or my sweater,
speared by the branch of a beachlog,
remain our private highwater mark.
There's nothing left, nothing to add,
for which the tide will not account:

fire, our awkward toes where
we yield, the periwinkles' slow track;
no matter how we want, beyond doubt,
to stay the tide or inform it, we
come in time to inform ourselves: we have
to follow it all the way out.

ADDING IT UP

My mind's eye opens before
the light gets up. I
lie awake in the small dark,
figuring payments, or how
to scrape paint; I count
rich women I didn't marry.
I measure bicycle miles
I pedaled last Thursday
to take off weight; I give some
passing thought to the point
that if I hadn't turned poet
I might well be some other
sort of accountant. Before
the sun reports its own weather
my mind is openly at it:
I chart my annual rainfall,
or how I'll plant seed if
I live to be fifty. I look up
words like "bilateral symmetry"
in my mind's dictionary; I consider
the bivalve mollusc, re-pick
last summer's mussels on Condon Point,
preview the next red tide, and
hold my breath: I listen hard
to how my heart valves are doing.
I try not to get going
too early: bladder permitting,
I mean to stay in bed until six;
I think in spirals, building
horizon pyramids, yielding to
no man's flag but my own.
I think a lot of Saul Steinberg:
I play touch football on one leg,
I seesaw on the old cliff, trying
to balance things out: job,
wife, children, myself.
My mind's eye opens before

my body is ready for its
first duty: cleaning up after
an old-maid Basset in heat.
That, too, I inventory:
the Puritan strain will out,
even at six a.m.; sun or no sun,
I'm Puritan to the bone, down to
the marrow and then some:
if I'm not sorry I worry,
if I can't worry I count.

WEAR

I hate how things wear out.

Not elbows, collars, cuffs;
they fit me, lightly frayed.

Not belts or paint or rust,
not routine maintenance.

On my own hook I cope
with surfaces: with all

that rubs away, flakes off, or fades
on schedule. What eats at me

is what wears from the in-
side out: bearings, couplings,

universal joints, old
differentials, rings,

and points: frictions hidden
in such dark they build

to heat before they come
to light. What gets to me

is how valves wear, the slow
leak in old circuitry,

the hairline fracture under
stress. With all my heart

I hate pumps losing prime,
immeasurable over-

loads, ungauged fatigue
in linkages. I hate

myself for wasting time
on hate: the cost of speed

came with the bill of sale,
the rest was never under

warranty. Five years
ago I turned in every

year; this year I rebuild
rebuilt parts. What hurts

is how blind tired I get.

DREAMSCAPE

On the steep road
curving to town, up
through spruce trees
from the filled-in canal,
there have been five houses, always.

But when I sleep
the whole left side of the blacktop
clears itself into good pasture.
There are two old horses,
tethered. And a curving row
of miniature bison, kneeling,

each with his two front hooves
tucked in neatly under the lip
of the asphalt. I am asleep.
I cannot explain it. I do not
want to explain it.

LANDFALL

Dreaming, offshore,
the low green mound of an island
I was about to land on,

I wake to dip
in a deep blue cup of a pond,
set in steep hills, far inland.

THIS DREAM

I climb up from this dream
the way, last fall, I finally
survived diving into a quarry:
by swimming, from dark, for
light as hard as pink granite.
They tell me I almost drowned.
Warm as I've grown, I'm
of no mind to remember.
As if from deep cold, I only know
to invite myself back: I tip
my eyes empty of sleep; then,
with the heel of each hand, I tap
the ringing out of each temple.
The small bells keep on.
If this is fever, I want it.
Everything's clear: the sun
has come back from nowhere,
and brought with it incalculable light.
This morning will not go away.
No more will I: I am in my element;
I baptize myself by breathing my name,
I give my new face to the sun.
I smile like everything, even
at me: I think I am perfectly mad:
I believe I will live forever.

HOW TO SEE DEER

Forget roadside crossings.
Go nowhere with guns.
Go elsewhere your own way,

lonely and wanting. Or
stay and be early:
next to deep woods

inhabit old orchards.
All clearings promise.
Sunrise is good,

and fog before sun.
Expect nothing always;
find your luck slowly.

Wait out the windfall.
Take your good time
to learn to read ferns;

make like a turtle:
downhill toward slow water.
Instructed by heron,

drink the pure silence.
Be compassed by wind.
If you quiver like aspen

trust your quick nature:
let your ear teach you
which way to listen.

You've come to assume
protective color; now
colors reform to

new shapes in your eye.
You've learned by now
to wait without waiting;

as if it were dusk
look into light falling:
in deep relief

things even out. Be
careless of nothing. See
what you see.

VERMONT

That narrow sea.
A hard riptide.
The waves take centuries
to break.

THE INCREDIBLE YACHTS

The incredible yachts: stays
and halyards geared to tension,
banks of winches on deck;
they blew into harbor
this evening: richly cruised men
wed to aluminum hulls
and fleet women: they raced
to get here. Once at anchor
in this stormed harbor,
in this indelible weather,
they bobbled the tide with
their empties: none of them
cared to know in truth
what harbor they were in.

PRIDES CROSSING

Born to Prides Crossing,
privately tutored; finished

at Foxcroft, engaged to
Groton and Harvard, wed

after the Coral Sea
and Midway; bride

to Treasury, wife
to Wall Street and mother

to Gracie Square, she
has been first mate

on three Bermuda races,
and is newly mistress

of one round-the-world
teak ketch. Aboard,

at her grandfather's
inlaid desk, far in

the Caribbean, she
times to her forty-

sixth birthday
her annual letter

to her last tutor.
Her hand is impeccably

North Shore italic:
Since Arthur's corporate

interests require him
to be in Aruba one day

and North of the Arctic
Circle the next, we

live somewhat separate
lives. Whit has been

asked to depart St. Paul's,
after drugs; we don't know

where he goes next. Jilly,
whom you last saw

the summer she was about
to start Chapin,

I have just now flown back
to New York to abort.

I have been hospitalized
myself, but am out

again for a third try.
At least I refuse

what my friends still
in Boston seem nowadays

to feast on: the sacrilege
of an easy Jesus.

Please do not
send me condolences;

I know you will not.
Her script slants

increasingly small: *I sit
to write you aboard*

*an anchored sailboat, with my
own name on her transom.*

She is perfectly furled. I
am afloat, the crew is ashore;

every halyard and sheet
is perfectly coiled. I sit

wondering, now, if life
will ever unbraid

itself. Or do
I mean unsnarl

itself? I know that you
cannot tell me this. . . .

But how, if it does,
will I know that it has?

PANIC

It is to be out
of familiar walls
with no place left
but the Halfway
House far up
the block: it is,
this first after-
noon, to carefully
ask your new self
for a walk beyond
the drugstore around
the block, but then
to have to refuse;
it is to remember
how trees grow out
of the sidewalk, to
figure how this time
to face him: the one
with hair like old vines,
who steps out of
nowhere, trying to
take you over, back
where he always
comes from; it is
having moved here
instead: here to
sleep, to learn
to get up: it is,
at supper the always
first night, to
try to ask for
the salt. And having it
passed, it's to weep.

LIKE A WOMAN

Like a woman
I loved, I say
words to the dark,
not to suffer.
Grown as I am,
I'm far from
immune: if I'm
in for it long
I want mind to
hold on, words in
my throat ready
to name it. Let
me keep fury
to stay against
pain; if it
is given me
to learn I mean
to know it all
the way, to bear
it like a woman.

IT IS BEING

... *the resolution of the will-to-being to detach itself from all determinate knowledge of being* ...

—Karl Jaspers

It is being offshore: nothing that's not horizon.
It is, beyond beacons, sailing alone.
Nothing, beyond one's compass, to point or warn.

It is, as necessity, knowing the old names for stars
blanked by cloud. To home on them is,
as it's given, to steer a singular course:

it is to navigate knowing that no port is home.
It is to assign one's self to the helm;
it is, offshore, repeating for sanity one's own name,

on watch beyond relief. It is standing watch
beyond hope of relief, weathering the blind fetch
of one's heart, and the crabbed set of one's mind.

It is tacking in fog. It is, of a stillness,
to fish with deep hooks. And, if they catch, to bless
with strange names from the masthead all you release.

Where there is nothing that's not horizon
it is, to ease thirst, sucking a fishbone.
It is being outside one's limits, the horizon's one man.

PHONE

Close to the road east of Machias,
a glass box under a telephone pole,
for miles of dark the one light left on.

Late, walked in out of rain,
a man in a blaze vest folds the door shut,
dials 0, and talks. The box inside

the glass box swallows his dime.
He dials again, pays again, listens,
and quits. Whatever it was he was after

the other end didn't come close.
The rain blows off; the light
stays on, precisely cast. Hooked

back up, the phone starts ringing.
The glass box vibrates, over and
over, then stops. Again, and

again it comes to nothing.
Hundreds of miles of dark.
The man walks back where he came from.

WORD

In a flat month
in a low field

I hit on a word
with just one

meaning. One.
It got to me,

hard. I stood
back up, grabbing

for balance; I
tried to hit

back. But it
meant it: no

matter what I
did nothing

would yield.
I tried old

levers: hope,
belief, love.

Earth would not
give, not for

the world. Not
one prospect

of any appeal.
That was final:

the word itself
would have the last

word; no way
around it, over,

or through. No
reason behind it.

Who, in God's name,
had what in mind?

I dug as deep as
my heart could stand.

WAYS

Gratefully,
with family around;
held to known hands:
the old way.

In a motel bathroom,
unable to get to
the phone.

While sirens flash,
watching blood channel;
trapped in the bite
of acetylene torches.

Fog and a mountain:
the warning lights pulse.
A belt in the gut.
All of you.

Feeling for handholds
on a sheer face,
cheek to cold stone.

The pain,
weighing tons,
shifting.

In prison,
the end of a sentence.

A red flannel shirt,
jogging, against
traffic.

Running uphill
through old films,
under orders.

Hearing the whistle
that notes
a trajectory.

Tubes at both ends;
paying for it.
Not even the nurses
can smile.

Cells eating cells:
childish arithmetic
followed by zeros.
Strangers: counting.
Relatives: counting.
Strangers and relatives,
counting. And counting.

Drunk, a half hour before sunrise.
Unable, for once, not
to reach for the gun.

Still listening for music.
A band at the corner:
turning maybe this way.
Or that.

Barely come out
of your doctor's brick office:

counting, already,
how friends will figure.

Figuring, newly,
the ways old friends managed.

Managing courage:
weeks of more tests.

OLD POEM

The train you took has taken all night.
East and North now, you wake to fog.
At the last platform a pick-up's waiting.

A kid drives, with headlights on,
focused down close against the blacktop.
No lights come out of the dark to meet you.

Maybe an hour: the road ends steep
on a wharf soft with fog. The fog is tidal:
an oak shows up, its bare limbs dripping.

A luncheonette trailer is parked on the wharf.
The fat woman offers you welcome coffee:
she slides back her window and slides out

the cup. She won't take your money;
she seems to imagine some family resemblance.
Or maybe she's sorry about your old limp.

Her nose is in the wrong part of her face.
She breathes like a foghorn. Her teeth
are as stained as your ebbed mug of coffee.

You, she says, you probably feel
like you just got to The Jumping-Off Place.
Just about then the fog gives up.

The oak stops dripping. The kid backs down,
to hitch his pick-up up to the trailer.
The lunch window locks. There's almost sun.

Now you can see both of the islands:
not far apart, but far miles out.
They look like stains on the pewter ocean;

save for the islands there's no horizon,
except between them there isn't a seam.
Not even a line between sky and water.

The fisherman down on the float says nothing.
He lets you cast off the boat yourself,
the boat you bought from an ad, sight unseen.

You find she mostly fires on all four.
She only skips sometimes. It doesn't matter.
The islands are straight down the bay,

straight out. There isn't a buoy in sight, or
a ledge. There's no sign of wind, no
other boat. Only the islands over your bow.

There isn't a seam, except between them.
The closer you head the clearer it comes.
What looked from land like old water, old sky,

between the islands divides to new color:
it looks now more like old tin and old lead:
the edge it took half your life to discover,
the edge you've figured all night to get over.

NATURAL HISTORY

March: a porcupine spent
March nights gnawing sap
from the blue spruce trunk;

he climbed two-thirds of
the cold March branches
before he bit into the bark.

A tree as tall as a house.
Now, midsummer, the sprucegum
still bleeds; like a root

cut quick by the blade
of a mower, the whole upper trunk
slowly gums up.

The porcupine trespasses
still, waddling toward evening
across the backyard like

a dirty quilled panda.
The two dogs might smile,
if they could. They hold back,

from experience. The porcupine,
fat as a garbage pail,
admits, to his nocturnal

seasons, no moral.
The spruce, through July,
dies without sorrow.

GRAFFITO

My father, 79,
died in his home bed
with no last word,
his jawbone frozen open.

Before the service
while the chimes said
nothing, I—afraid I
might die the same way—

ran to a mens' room
deep in the chapel.
Letting go, I read
pencil on marble:

Time is nature's way
of preventing
everything
from happening all at once.

Father, forgive
my unforgiving mouth:
I sang how those words sang,
I felt the whole stall dance.

WATCH

The hand keeps sweeping across
its seconds; after a minute

the minute changes, number
on number the new hours fall.

Our Roman numerals
glow in the dark

like initials carved
in space. Now and again,

near dawn, we admit to
the domed house we live in:

we allow enough of ourselves
to deny we've been proofed

against tears, or built
resistant to shock.

There is no end to the lies
we devise to live by,

or the limits we claim to die for.
When our bodies fail

we claim the clear glass
of our souls is immortal,

we name ourselves
as deserving heirs,

we light small candles
and wish. Or promise.

Better we name, in true order,
commanders deceased overseas

in the Punic Wars; better,
before old tides and new,

we for once try silence,
love starlight, believe

in morning, and come in our fields
to lean on the morning wind.

STRIP

Möbius knew: he
figured it out:

this complex plane
does not, by

any equation,
add up to

zero.
It happens barely:

after the turn,
opposites start

to connect,
the event

becomes an act
of relief:

a continuous
map of how, in

half-turning,
a man

can surface to
change; he thumbs

his way home
the long way

around, from
where he is

to where he
intends: he

finds himself
turning

back into
himself.

MOMENT

The old sting.   Dead.
The bee.   Honey
here on the tongue.

Moment on moment
each moment blooms.
The moment flowers
whether or not
we want it, whether
or not we let it
occur to us.
Nothing happens,
still, without
our knowing. We think,
but what matter?
Once the moment
is over its wild
persistence goes
to seed. Once
and once, over
and over, the present
gives itself up:
the past cannot
remember the future
does not yet know.

The dead sting.   A be-
coming other.   Now.
Here on the tongue.

LIVES

I

A far coast.
The dark come down early.
Down over the hill, the harbor.
The old heaved sidewalk. By nine
not even a houselight still on.

Under the one corner streetlight
two new figures: they stand strange.
And now another. No car, out of nowhere.
Then here, this corner.

We talk.
        Strange
so familiar: after
a funeral in Halifax once.
It's true. I even imagine
I know the third one.

The draggers start bunting the spiles,
the tide must have turned.

We go down in the dark to see.

Against the pull of the ebb
there are fish who sound small,
flipping the surface.
           Fish
after fish.
        We listen,
watching the dark.
As if it weren't winter
we swing legs over
the edge of the wharf.

The scallop season opens
at midnight, the men already collecting
under the single light.

What a life.

We haul each other back up.

II

What a life.

Seasons of leaves, interstices
of pure light. Holy days:
solstice and equinox; cold
coming clear and tipping
the balance. We grow
to be old.

The store, the mail, stopping
for gas; mornings of evening
invitations.
                Everyone lives
as though no one knew.

III

Driven home late:
                        same old Chevy, same
kid-argument.
                        High on headlights, a deer
settles it: sprung almost across the road
in one leap.
                Almost.
                        The curve,
the centrifugal pull of a sixpack.

                        The power line arcs.
All down the line
all the lights
go out.
                        Or a dog, the next noon,
in a first spit
of snow. He goes
for the joy of it, running

the wind.   Then, when it
stops, the wind of quick cars. Car
after car.
                    Then a gull,
headed crosswind.
                         The driver gets out
and walks back.
                         The blood of the world
floods the dog's mouth.

                              People who know better
cruise after church,
                         spotting the sites;
close to bared apples, they stop
by the Grange where deer browse.
                                   Four days to wait,
                                   a short season
this year: headlights at dusk
flick down the woods-roads. Guns
racked against the backwindows
of pick-ups.
                    Back in the store
the men talk of bearscat.

IV

His wife and son left, a boy
in a loft far inland sleeping off
grief.
          Mice. Winter squash.

He gets up in the cold to do *t'ai chi*.
The first time since July.
Everything in him quivers.

I am learning to be quiet, to listen,
to balance, to try for the balance of us all
whether to continue or to cease.
Behind him the wind clear-cuts the hillside.

Leaves at his feet, the ground frozen,

he stretches, feels his muscles remember each other,
balances, holds, and eases.

I ask myself now as I look at these I's
if there is something to be said
past the realization that there is nothing
to be said.

Parsnips, turnips, hard squash, the root
shapes. A whole spring catalogue
come to bear on the floor of the loft.
They weigh, grown to nightmare.

It is cold in the loft, and when
I do sleep it is sound.

Beyond sleep, in the hardwood valley
where deer in their season
will finally come down,

a hundred Presidents hang racked
on a single tree, each
like a small boy's school-window moon.

I think of the places
we loved. The shore, tides,
the years.
       Moved, they've
gone far. Moved, the boy
writes his letter

much love
       and walks all the way
into Conway to mail it.
         Miles
of valley carved by the river,
whole geologic ages.
         Old foothills.
He feels them close:
         millions
of rains on the ridges.

V

The first hard freeze, three calm nights without let-up.
This third morning, black ice:
                              the surface
flowered with frost, the whole marsh frozen into
a stillness:
                    the windless channels give way
to islands of marshgrass, bleached ninetails;
                                            the reaches
edge behind larch to maple; beyond their silver,
whole horizons of fir.
                          We sit on mittens,
lacing old skates.
                        I watch you happen to smile,
wondering how we ever came
                                to love.
Next to the outlet, a big pipe under a country road,
the black ice skims to nothing;
                                    wondering where
the source is, we skate a surface
                                    barely safe:
the new ice sinks and swells as it takes up
our weight;
                  reports crack ahead of us,
blazing our passage, mapping it.
                                    We skate to a drum
we half create, run out of wind
                                and stop, still.
The sky's brittle.
                        Airbubbles pumped out of nowhere
freeze under our feet in mid-ice:
                                    schools of loosed stars,
small planets,
                    and moons come to nought.
Surveyors of space
                        new to us, we focus down
through galaxies
                      to eelgrass waving in soft currents;
beetles small as a dot
                          swim at large under
the planets.

We slide a foot toward what an old man wrote
the week before he died:
we live, we have
        to live, on
                insufficient
evidence.

It's true: brightly stilted, surfaced on dense shallows,
we steady each other by
             studying a slow green dance:
newts and frogs
        tunneled into the silt,
maybe with crayfish and perch
              covered by last summer's layers:
planaria, husks of dragonflies.
            Through the ice,
darkly, we half see
        how the heron lives; frozen out,
the ducks and he
        took off for God knows where.
The chickadee in the hackmatack whistles his calling across
the marsh, a small solace
        where we skate
              filled
with an absence.
        Who knows what we did to help? Who
        knows, ever, how to give what's due?
It's true:
      we never know
           a life
             enough. . . .

The black ice cracks and holds:
you pump off hard
to the beaver house
        your far eye just discovered.
Now you shout back
        through first thin snow
what only the beaver
can hear, or only
the pickerel and hornpout
        nosed into mud,

or the painted turtle we'll come back to count

next spring.

Close to the source

I ease across flexible ice

to catch you:

opening ourselves

between ninetails and snow

we come close

and hug:

lives

we barely know, lives

we keep wanting

to know.

VI.

NOT TO TELL LIES

He has come to a certain age.
To a tall house older than he is.
Older, by far, than he ever will be.
He has moved his things upstairs, to a room
which corners late sun. It warms a schooner model,
his daughter's portrait, the rock his doctor brought him
back from Amchitka. When he looks at the rock he thinks Melville;
when he touches the lichen he dreams Thoreau. Their testaments
shelve the inboard edge of the oak-legged table he writes on.
He has nailed an ancestor's photograph high over his head.
He has moored his bed perpendicular to the North wall;
whenever he rests his head is compassed barely west
of Polaris. He believes in powers: gravity, true
North, magnetic North, love. In how his wife
loved the year of their firstborn. When-
ever he wakes he sees the clean page in
his portable. He has sorted life out;
he feels moved to say all of it,
most of it all. He tries
to come close, he keeps
coming close: he has
gathered himself
in order not
to tell
lies.

Aside from the life
I live inside it,
this room is nothing.
Nothing invades it.
I try to figure: I
am more vital than it;
that is my virtue: not
in my own life to live
as if nothing
were more important.

WORDS FOR THE ROOM

Today's a long season after Thanksgiving.
I got up early, let out the dogs, and ate.
I've got almost four almost-right poems,

and one quick typewriter set before me,
plus a silvery Piels Real Draft, already
half empty at my left hand. I sit

on the right hand of Saint Jarrell, despairing,
trying to mind an old heart that is, in spite
of itself, almost full. I love my children,

I'm stunned by my grandson, renewed by my wife.
I almost have poems. And, to complete them,
hundreds of words, a whole dark roomful to choose from.

Words for the room: a new ceiling, a door.
That's all, they're all, between me and the world;
nothing but choice, nothing save will:

infinitives, relative objects. I can feel,
I can name, what I have to decide: I mean
if I mean to revise my whole life.

In this gray depression
I try to sleep off, or
wake from, nothing connects.
Nothing gets to me. In that
there is nothing to say,
I have to begin with nothing.
In that there is nothing
to feel, there's nothing
I'd better question. I find
myself far into mid-life
willing at last to begin.

FALLING APART

The windows stay.
The clapboards go wavy.
The high branches look
to belong to the elm.

It's inside things
don't arrive right: how
far from my good eye
this left fist is; or
this swelled thumb. How long
my neck has refused to
hold up its head. Parts
of me disincline; I lean
in a lot of directions,
all without compass.

There isn't fog, but
it's gray all day: gray
in the elms' old elbows,
gray in my bowels. Cracks
in the clapboard want paint.
My hand thinks my head
needs more room on the sill.
There are holes where some-
body took out the nails.

Only the windows stay.

FLINCHING

Crossing from where he has been
to where he even less wants to go,

hollow of sleep, faced by the moon,
he feels animals in him eat at their reins.

Marooned between lines of opposing traffic,
he tries to get off the island ledge:

he prays to Kochab, and wakes without sun,
the morning opera already howling.

Distrusting the natives two valleys west,
he steals along clamflats; waves

breed waves twice as high as his head:
wherever he moves is over the edge.

OUT OF THE ORDINARY

Halfway south, in one
of hundreds of would-be cities
ending in -ville,
              he looked at dusk
out his motel window: a blackwoman
gardened the narrow strip between
the cementblock walls
                    where he'd sleep
and where her own clapboards
faded toward white. A dog's lope beyond,
across the sideroad,
              a slow-pitch game
was beginning under the long-stemmed lights.
Over their flowering, nighthawks stunted;
the thinnest possible moon
                  was just making up.
Out of the ordinary, too tired to rest,
he stood and looked: he looked and looked
for the joy of it.

Noam was in intensive care when he came to.
The truck hit the taxi, the taxi jumped the curb,
sideswiped him and felled his wife, then twisted
back at him.
                    Heigh-ho, the dairy-o,
she'd just gone out to buy milk . . .

Noam saw the replay before the nurse came on:
Don't worry, *she said,* you're going
to be all right. Nothing
is going to happen.
I know, *Noam said,* it already has.

MATTER

No matter what you do
or don't, or imagine,

the tree you live by
is bound to come down.

Maybe not in your lifetime.
Without doubt in its own.

A SLOW BREAKER

Washing on granite
before it turns
on itself, away

from every horizon
it fetched from,
this clear green wash,

the flashing, cold,
specific gravity of it,
calls the eye down

to what we thought to
look into, to all we
cannot see through.

RECALL

Father,
    Without you, I drift off at work
with a dream you must have slept with
for years:
        that spanking-new '34 Chevy
parked at the top of the steep cement ramp
in the brick garage where you always bought cars
in the town I could never grow up in.

I went with you the day they delivered:
the cream wheels, the plush smell, the braided cord for
a laprobe—a car I've had stored so long
I forgot it.
        I barely wake now,
cold Aprils after your dying, to this green car
mother paid for, this dream I've slept on
for hundreds of seasons, this face in the rear-view mirror
that looks more like yours
than my own;
        I own to it now:
the way I have to reclaim what I've left,
the way I need to get myself back.

His nurse, at bedside, said What is it?
Nothing, *Noam said,* it's nothing.

He heard her keep saying I want to know.
No, *he said,* nobody wants to.

I tell you I do. I want
to know. Where does it hurt?

It doesn't, it's
nothing, nothing at all.

You're trying to cry, it's got
to be hurting.

I tell you it's nothing,
nothing is all.

FOG

Winded, drifting to rest.
                    I'm rowing
between islands, between pewter water
and a gauze I'm unwinding that winds back
behind me in my flat wake.
                    At the tip
of each oar small vortices whorl
at each stroke's end.
                    If I looked down through
I could see Stephen who swam for his friend
on his eighth birthday. Or Mr. Ames,
swept overboard at daybreak, racing
big seas off Greenland. Or his boys
who went after him.
                    They were my heroes
the June I was nine. It's different now:
with no horizon, with the end
of the century coming up,
                    I'm rowing
where measure is lost, I'm barely moving,
in a circle of translucence that moves with me
without compass.
                    I can't see out or up into;
I sit facing backwards,
                    pulling myself slowly
toward the life I'm still trying to get at.

Nothing is sure.
Nothing in me
approaches nothing
constantly; though
I approach nothing
at a constant rate,
the process, as
we close, seems
to accelerate.

RATES

A caterpillar, long
beyond summer, crossing
the blacktop
east of Machias

  Copernicus Leonardo Luther

a fingerling headed
downstream, in
an eddy

  Galileo Shakespeare Newton

pinwheeling out in
M-101, a white dwarf dead
before history was born

  Bach Voltaire Diderot Hume

the black mark spun
through the meter down cellar,
a bulb left on in the attic
all winter

  Kant Mozart Blake

forsythia, barely
unfolded, out on
the outskirts
of Gander

  Darwin Marx Van Gogh

a tern, its beak
quick with herring,
flying up through current to
sun

Freud Picasso Einstein

a far gun: while
smoke announces
something has started, air
withholding
its tall report.

GENERATION

A bald fifty-some,
                    shaving in
his dead father's
nickel-plated
                    extensible mirror
(patented 1902),
the father, stripped
                    to bathe, notes
his bare grandson
studying again, from
                    four-year-old
eye-level, the old
primary stem,
                    hanging out
from the apple-
pouch where he
                    remembers his father's,
presiding over
a wad of wirehair.
                    He shaves considering
all the trouble.

We used to say Nothing's
too good for our kids.

Now we don't know what to say.

Nothing seems to be good enough
for them. If everything isn't
just right, nothing will do.

THE YOUNG

They keep doing it.
                    Missing
the curve.
                    Three, already,
in just this one year.
                              The same
stretch, three different lives.
A telephone pole, a tree,
a stonewall.
                    The headlights hit
before the car rolls.
                              They keep
doing it.
              Too much or too little,
in wrong combinations, too late.
Or too early.
                    They keep missing
the curve.
                    The siren.
                              And in
a dark house the darkness through
hundreds of nights after the phone
begins its blind ring.

DRAGGING

A whole week. Out of
the north all day.

A dry cold. The wind
clean as split oak.

Dark islands, dark as
the march of whitecaps.

Under hills hard on
the shoreline: churches,

settlements, planted
like bones. Out here,

the boat on good marks,
we let the wire out:

the drag plunges and
tugs. First light to

first dark, we tow, dump,
set, tow. Numb to what

cuts our hands, we set,
tow, dump, mend; tow until

dark closes down. We clean
the catch heading in

through dark to the thin
walls of our lives, grown

numb to the wind, numb
to the dark, to all we've

dragged for and taken,
shells returned to

that other dark that
weighs the whole bottom.

Durward: setting his trawl
for haddock, and handlining cod
a halfmile east of Seal Island,

twelve miles offshore in fog.
Then his new engine went out.
A Rockland dragger spotted him,

two days later, drifting drunk
off Mount Desert Rock. He was
down to his last sixpack.

After they towed him back in,
Ordway kept asking him what
—those two days—he'd been thinking.

Nothin. I thought about nothin.
That was all there was to it.
Ord said, Y'must've thought something.

Nope, I thought about nothin.
You know what I thought,
I thought fuckit.

HERE

There
is which way the wind blows
and how:
        with what strength
and fetch,
          but the choice is
in us
      we think whether
               to search
out into it,
        and, if we do, what
course to set:

        to beat into it,
the familiar
         semblance of achievement,
feeling
      sure
         resistance
to all
      we hope to make good;

or simply reaching
             across it,
the fastest possible passage;
that, or
      easing off all
          the way,
even
    with luck
         skill earns
the surest
      risk,
        the closest to
rolling
     out of control;

           the choice is
not

            in the cabin which barely
lends us shelter,
                        the choice is in us
in us:
            what we have heart for,
            to what we are equal:

                        the planet
long since gathered torque
                  pulsing
                  the wind this way:
                                    as if
                  we could choose
                                    as if
                  there were choice.

POEM FOR THE TURN
OF THE CENTURY

Wars ago, wars ago
               this dawn,
the sun come up under cloud,
up and into,
                  men waded ashore
on some June beach
to die.
            At war again
with ourselves
at the century's turn
                   again
we've set sail:
the shore we keep closing on
                      comes clear
through the glass:
on the edge of a village
                     steeped with windmills
people appear
to hill their crop
               with no weapon
beyond a hoe.
In the sinking distance
                 we hailed from,
miles aft,
as the sun
            comes over
the cloudbank,
light takes
            the residual islands
like a wreath
laid on the sea.

When the nurse finally brought in his bedpan,
Noam felt as certain as Luther of wisdom:

Diarrhea spelled backwards, *he told her,*
is, practically, air raid.

Whadidyasay? *she said.* Nothing,
Noam said, I said nothing.

CALENDAR

Two months after
the birth of her
June child, she found

in her neighbor's
backyard that she
couldn't talk. She

ran inside to
write on a pad
don't worry, and

found she couldn't
write. New Year's night
she'd found a mole

grown wild on her
arm. Too many
lifetimes after

her neighbor held
her, her brother-
in-law came for

the child. She
shouted him out
the backdoor: *Look*

at me, I'm a
corpse. . . . He ran.
She came that close.

The dark comes down
in white rooms where it
settles nothing.

The dead go on their own way

OSSIPEE: NOVEMBER

The dark fold of the land:
steeped hills settling
a pond between them.

Black ice on the pond.
Glacial boulders in brooks
holding snow. Halfway up

the horizon, snowsqualls
tall against sun. A tree points,
spare on the clearcut spine

of a mountain. Wherever
it was the lightplane went down
won't unlock until April.

Ord kept asking:
How'd it happen?
How'd he do it?

Everyone said
nobody knew.

Durward said,
Noam used to say
he'd been some
to a shrink . . .

Jesus, *Ordway*
said, he was
a shrink. You got
to go to one
to be one. It's
like signing-on
with a church.

All's I know,
Durward said,
Noam must've been
some good doctor.
He had himself
a built-in
shit detector.

Finest kind, *Ord said.*
But maybe that's what
clogged him up. Maybe
he couldn't stand
all he knew. Maybe he
didn't have any way
left to feel. A man
sits all day
on the edge of nothing,
after a while he
gets numb and falls in.

SYNTAX

Short of words in that quick dark
where there was nothing between them,

he longed, in her, for some light verb
which, if she could, would ease him.

Nothing is given.
Nothing is unforgiving.

STILL LIFE

The new-cut key on the blue-paint table.
Your place now. The third-floor door,
the stairwell turn no bed
could get up through. But did.

After you get the boy to sleep
you sit at the blue-paint table.
Tea with nothing. No milk, no honey.

Against the table: the small brass shine.

By the time you lie back down
on the same old mattress
you've decided: strip the blue paint off,
bring the whole thing back to natural.
That's what you promise yourself you'll do.

Do for yourself. For Christmas.

SORTING IT OUT

At the table she used to sew at,
he uses his brass desk scissors
to cut up his shirt.
                    Not that the shirt
was that far gone: one ragged cuff,
one elbow through;
                    but here he is,
cutting away the collar
she long since turned.
                    What gets to him finally,
using his scissors like a bright claw,
is prying buttons off:
                    after they've leapt,
spinning the floor, he bends
to retrieve both sizes:
                    he intends to
save them in some small box; he knows
he has reason to save; if only he knew
where a small box
                    used to be kept.

OLD MAN

This is a dream I needed.

I wake in my own old room
toward morning, lying next to the knees
of a girl—a young mother—born
in the milltown miles upriver.
Kneeling beside me, smiling,
she lets her long hair shelter me from
every view of myself. Except, out the dormer window,
the town's last elm.

I adore you
I tell her.
I know, she says,
with you I am quiet.

This is a sleep I am lucky to wake from.

By the time I walk down over the hill
for the *News,* she is opening her store.
She turns in the doorway, her son in arms,
and smiles. I nod and smile, trusting myself
not to say I adore her, trusting her
to dream what I have not said.

No matter how I feel,
I am of several minds.

Nothing I think is as sure
as my mind's several voices.

MARY'S, AFTER DINNER

Both hands talking, raised to shoulder height,
the left uptilted with a Lucky Strike,
the right still doubled down, inside of smoke,
across an opposite heart:
                              the argument is nothing,
nothing after all . . .
                              . . . all August that we've drunk,
made talk of, dined on, drawn back from,
then come back to sip;
                              the evening settled,
dearly, in your hands, the room
moves to the logic of your smile:
sitting full-face, unsurrender'd,
you say whole strophes from *Anon.,*
the truest poet of all;
                              more telling
than we knew, their measure
opens us to speak:
                              before the fire
your calendar has lit, brilliant
for the moment, we let words raise us
by their power:
                              we hear
our language validate our lives.

THINKING ABOUT HANNAH ARENDT

(1906–1975)

The kitchen stove wood-ash
I took out this morning,
to dress the snowfield
that covers the garden.

The ashwood I've blazed
to fell before dark:
a whole grove to go,
to limb and twitch out,
to yard and fit; then,
after all, let season.

This present fire.
This kitchen oven.

The cigarette smoke you inhaled, held deep,
and let drift, displaced
in Maine, telling
your fear in being a Jew
landing alone in
Damascus. At home
with how slowly
iron heats, with
how strange to
myself I am, I sit
by a stove as dark as
the mourning you wore
against snow. I lean
to the exquisite warmth
of your sadness, your
intricate face:
              your eyes clear
with a reason dear beyond reason.

THIS DAY AFTER YESTERDAY
ROBERT TRAILL SPENCE LOWELL (1917–1977)

I

This day after yesterday.

Morning rain small on the harbor,
nothing that's not gray.

I heard at Hooper's, taking the Plymouth in
for brakes. Out from behind
his rolltop desk, Ken said, "*Ra*dio says
a *co*lleague of yours died. Yessir,
*died. Low*ell. Wasn't he your friend?"

Yesterday blazed, the Bay full of spindrift and sun.
If you'd looked down from your Ireland plane
I could have shared you twelve seals upriver,
seven heron in Warm Cove, and
an early evening meteor.
                            If I'd said such portents,
you would have flattened me with prepschool repartee,
your eyes owl'd out:
                    "And a poet up a fir tree . . ."

II

That's how friendship went.

At least this summer,
this last summer:
                    home,
almost home.

Ulysses come up over the beachstones,
shuffling with terrible age. We hugged and
parted, up the picnic field,
lugging tens of summers.

III

You wanted women, mail, praise.
What men thought of what you'd conquered.
Beyond the irony of fame, the honor due
to how a poet suffers: the brilliance of first drafts,
the strophe tinker'd into shape, a life
in twelve right lines come almost whole.
You were voluntarily committed: you sweat-out hours
to half-know what the day's poems came to.

Who knows what they did? Or,
by your dying, have?

                Who knows what word
                you were bringing home?
                You, bridging marriages,
                Ulysses into Queens and through.

                An almost final draft
                for your collected life,
                your unrevisable last poem.

IV

You were a trying man, God knows.
Over drinks, or after, your wit mauled,
twice life sized: like your heroic mattress-chest.

Manic, you were brutal. The brightest boy
in school, the school's most cruel monitor,
you wrenched skin, or twisted arms, as if

Caligula were just. Of those who never made
a team, you were Captain; to them, life-long,
you were Boston-loyal. Guilt in excess

was your subject, not your better nature.
For sheer guts you had no peer. Sane,
you almost seemed God's gentlest creature.

V

Jesus, how death gets to us . . .

On the Common, just this week,
they've jacked up Harriet Winslow's house,
all the front sills gone.

And on the sea-side of the Barn
you wrote in, the bulkhead
finally gave way to the tide.

And then the giving-way you,
like Agee, never got to write:
a poet in a New York cab . . .

VI

Weighed by your dying,
Cal, I find myself

much wanting. How could
I dread you less, or

love you more? Left
time, I try to write

old summers back, as if
you'd never maddened

my perspective. More
in misery than love,

I have your life
by heart. Without you,

I am easier and less:
the planet grays,

the village rot
you left eats through

another step, the Bay
that was our commonplace

is flatter . . .

VII

Everything about me
sags: my body tells

my disbelief its
own mortal story.

I meant to write
a different poem:

>   *A seal to tides.*
>   *A heron lifted off.*
>   *A meteor.*

No. If poems
can be believed,
better how
time conjugates:

>   *day by day,*
>   *day after day,*
>   *this day after yesterday* . . .

a dog with flattened
ears, lying on

old dung, lifts
his muzzle, the lame

best that he can,
to welcome his

old master
home.

>   *May all such ghosts attend*
>   *your spirit, now. May it,*
>   *with them, be lighter.*

GATHERING GREENS
DONALD DIKE (1920–1978)

In thin snow
blown inland
from sea, all

afternoon I've
tracked into
the woods after

cedar, hemlock,
and spruce. I've
come across

mouse-print,
fox-sign, and
deer run to where

the old dark
spends the night.
I've been here

before, but not
so far in; not
beside partridge

in blow-down, not
to the deeryard
in snow. I need

to learn to
protect myself,
as any animal

must. I try
to learn with
myself to be

gentle: to wait
until light
for the first

shadow to
point me out
to the coast.

LICHENS

Close to the point a mile upriver
where nuclear waste begins
to waste, close to the end

of the century, the coast weathers
before its next weather: March,
the primary colors still sky,

ocean, granite, spruce, snow;
and in a noon clearing, a knoll
in woods the British once stormed,

the lichens as the sun finds them:
nonflowering pioneer plants,
a low mix of algae and fungi,

they name themselves: Toad Skin
or Map Lichen written on rock,
Reindeer rampant through moss,

British Soldiers in log rot,
and Pale Shield lichen against
the northside of hemlock, rooted

where redcoats fell for nothing,
where man availeth not, where
the wind veers quiet as if March

could prime new life, the lichens
still, the lichens hold,
close to the bone of the planet.

THOREAU NEAR HOME

Seasick off Cape Ann, by moonlight,
on the night boat bound for Portland,
he took a week by mailcoach
tacking inland in hope
of some new school that wanted teaching.
No one listened save an Oldtown Indian.

May 13: looking east from Belfast for
some fairer weather, he booked passage
for Castine, an eight-mile reach, aboard
the sailboat *Cinderilla*.

He found the harbor full: coasters, one
square-rigger, shallops, pulling-boats.
Walking Argyle Street's steep hill, he
step by step rested his whole frame,
that each moment might abide. White clapboard,
spires, and cupolas claimed his eye.
A boy named Philip Hooke pointed to
Fort George, meadowy ramparts crowning
the peninsula. A war ago, boys
hardly men were posted here to die.

No, no teaching offered here.
By another spring, he thought, I
may be a Greenland whaler or
mail-carrier in Peru. All answers
being in the future, day answering
to day, he studied, into evening, how
merchants and how seamen paced their lives.
Bright as roadside shadblow
the night came fresh with stars.
He stayed the night at Deborah Orr's.

Captain Skinner, on the morning packet
back to Belfast, kept the poems of Burns
shelved in his cabin. As strewn clouds cleared,

201

Thoreau took the deck and looked back at the cliffs
that had not heard of Emerson.
The village shone.

Within a week, Thoreau would be home;
two months from now he would be twenty-one.
He stood watch on Castine, the farthest east
he ever sailed. He thought back to the *Iliad* and Homer;
he found the day fit for eternity, and saw
how sunlight fell on Asia Minor.

By self-definition
I cannot measure
a particle of myself,
not even the wavelength
of my own shadow. How
can I shape what I feel?
Beyond naming names,
nothing can help.
I learn my limits,
I write what I can;
I didn't become
a poet for nothing.

TOOLS

To get a handle on how
the day may work: a wedge

to split chunks off, a bar
with good purchase

to bring them home; saws,
next, to rip out grain,

then crosscut what lengths
come to: the grandfather head

of one man's hammer;
the day's ash hung

by spokeshave and rasp
to fit the arc

it strikes
against morning's turning:

by evening maybe
something to

show for: words
that name what shape

day took, or
one may still imagine.

EATON'S BOATYARD

To make do, making a living:
                    to throw away nothing,
practically nothing, nothing that may
come in handy;
                    within an inertia of caked paintcans,
frozen C-clamps, blown strips of tarp, and
pulling-boat molds,
                    to be able to find,
for whatever it's worth,
                    what has to be there:
the requisite tool
                    in this culch there's no end to:
the drawshave buried in potwarp,
chain, and manila jibsheets,
                    or, under the bench,
the piece that already may fit
                    the idea it begins
to shape up:
                    not to be put off by split rudders,
stripped outboards, half
a gasket, and nailsick garboards:
                    to forget for good
all the old year's losses,
                    save for
what needs be retrieved:
                    a life given to
how today feels:
                    to make of what's here
what has to be made
to make do.

Nothing is more than
simple absence: no father,
no tree to lean on,
no current to ride,
no rock off the shore
to feel a toe down to.

Nothing, at bottom,
is to have nothing
at heart: no self left
who will hear one's
other self speak, no
sense that relates
to another sense,
feeling nothing
permeate everything.

Nothing has meaning.
Nothing means what
it says: the acute
presence of absence:
the who I am not,
the where God isn't,
the void the dead leave,
the when I am dead.

Nothing is infinite absence
invading the finite truth
of my life: my own absence
from years of mornings,
the emptying-out of self
I cannot avoid, the void
of not being I cannot
learn to believe in.

BUILDING HER

Wood: learning it:
               feeling the tree
shiver the helve, feeling the grain
resist the saw, feeling for grain
with adze and chisel, feeling the plank
refuse a plane, the voyage of sap
still live in the fiber;
               joining wood:
scarfing it, rabbeting keel and sternpost,
matching a bevel, butting a joint
or driving a trunnel:
               whatever fastens
the grain, the grain lets in, and binds;

let wood breathe or keep wood briny,
wood will outlive generations:

working wood, a man learns how
wood works:
               wood comes and goes
with weather or waves; wood gives:

come to find right grain for timbers,
keelson, stem, a man can feel
how wood remembers:
               the hull will
take to sea the way the tree knew wind.

Nothing answers to
nothing. Nothing
else. The question
is not how to outlive
life, but how
—in the time we're
possessed by—to face
the raw beauty of being.

DAYRISE

At first light I hear miles of silence.
Except for the First Selectman's snowtires
snuffling up Main Street, it's Sunday-quiet;

half awake, knowing that deer season's done,
I dream of does wounded, bedded in spruce groves.
And bucks downed in the bog, who had last night

to give up. I doze with Han-Shan, the old T'ang drunk,
who took to Cold Mountain after the capital
turned down his poems. The woodfire's dying;

I get myself up to stoke it, rewrite night-notes
next to the stove, and wake my wife. After breakfast,
before I try to home-in on today's unwritten poem,

we go out into winter to fell next year's wood:
with her small ax and my stuttering saw, we cut near the bog,
on the low spruce crown of the woodlot we call Cold Knoll.

SOUNDINGS

Change   that cannot
be changed.   Who
we were: who knows
what was true?   Or is.
We used to dream islands.
Now we think woodlots.

You haven't touched the piano
for years, for years I believed
you'd give my words music.

Change   the old constant
change: where morning sun was,
how fog comes in over Cape Rosier:
for years and years over and over
in streams, wisps, bankings, whole clouds
at a time.   This afternoon again
it was different.   You, going gray,
have grown new, you've touched me
to lean to see how you feel.

Changing   what moves us
changes: we move with fog
into new coves and settle ourselves
in peninsular woods.   As I go
to fell oak I can hear your hands
gaining their way back up the piano.

BEFORE SLEEP

The day put away before bed,
the house almost closed before night.

By the time I walk out over the knoll,
down the steep Main Street

that dead-ends in the sea,
the village has put out its lights.

The winter stars are turned up over
the tide, a tide so quiet the harbor

holds stars. The planet holds.
Before the village turns over in sleep,

I stand at the edge of the tide,
letting my feet feel into the hillside

to where my dead ancestors live.
Whatever I know before sleep

surrounds me. I cannot help know.
By blood or illness, gossip or hope,

I'm relative to every last house.
Before I climb home up the hill, I hold:

I wait for myself to quiet, breathing
the breath of sleepers I cannot help love.

THE HOUSE IN THE TREES

Within an island of trees in the space of nature
it is barely there.
                          Hard to discover,
strange to remember the way.
                                 The house in the trees
is constantly being arrived at.
It conforms to the hillside, it receives light
as a guest. There is no wind in the trees,
but the house trembles
                          on the verge of being lived in.
It wants paint
                to define its existence, it takes on color
containing the air around it. Walls emerge
in every advent of weather,
                               a house in the process
of being built, of building:
Cézanne said
                I am its consciousness.
Waiting it out, he watched himself making it happen:
within an island of trees, a human
plenitude at the center. This is the house
every day he painted
                       he took to sleep and woke up in,
barely clothed in the freedom of knowing
before it could ever be done
he would have, finally, to leave it.

VII.

TO THINK

Suppose the astronomers right:
the original bang, the cosmos

expanding: a fraction less
expansion, the universe would

have collapsed; a fraction more,
gravity wouldn't have held its

stars. But luck, if it was,
made possible biota. We began

to evolve toward wonder: man
on earth. But what if we alone

are conscious, if outside us
there is no measure of our

complexity? Who else could
believe the ways we invent

to see ourselves across time,
to hear across distance, to fire

ourselves into unbreathable sky?
Fire stations, curtainrods,

dogs, zoos, the traffic
down school steps to recess,

the beds we make kids in, the streams
we dam; who, in a cosmos

empty of us, could account for
twi-night baseball or why

we bid Two No Trump or name
a trout fly Blue Cupsuptic?

If only we diagram stars,
and dream them into daylight

as signs of our meaning, as
proof of intent, or hope of

reason beyond our own, what
reason have we to imagine

that anyone might imagine us?
Who, for Christ's sake?

Until we invented God,
who could believe? We love

to believe, we have to believe
we love. But to think:

after we go, in the last
millisecond when boats,

Chicago, tulip beds,
wolves caged in Stuttgart,

incubators, and condoms
all blow, that the planet

will be beyond wonder, without
wonder what we were ever about.

HERE, THERE

Sky the color of early ice.
Wind off the pole.
Morning shapes itself
in immaculate drifts.
Late daylight: I'm
only half up;
everything's close to
zero, or five below,
under an arctic high.
I breakfast trying
to figure my marriage:
my wife is out across
the Pacific, by now
maybe miles above Wake,
her Nembutal probably not
yet working, her eyes
still blurred with new stars.
I try to get a hold
of myself: I take
the old globe out
of a closet, and look up
names from old wars:
*Wake   Eniwetok   Tinian
Saipan*. Maybe, now,
she's about to let down
over Guam, already
tomorrow by my time.
It's time to get on
with the rest of the day.
But today already
begins to escape me:
I can't figure out
where the sun went.
Me and my four new
felt-tip pens—I
spent a year's colors
charting strange time zones,

that long half-morning, half
yesterday, before
she finally took off.
Even now I can't plot
the slippage: sleep
between us, the screwed-up
clock I forgot to wind;
whatever it is,
across the dateline,
that keeps on gaining or
getting lost. I try
to remember how love
used to work: Sundays,
summers, places we used
to live. Today, here,
the dogs I let out
already want in: they
scratch at the door
for a hundredth time.
Icicles trim their jaws.
Getting myself up
to shave, I think—
in the mirror—I look
like an aspirin ad.
My stomach hurts.
I jam my hand as
deep as possible into
the Marianna Trench
of my last year's
Christmas pajamas,
feeling far down for
what warmth she's
left in these old
private parts.

GROWING UP IN KANKAKEE

Irrevocably the day begins our toward each other
turnings.
        Nurses at their small-town stations in cities
beyond belief, looking for sun at corridor's end
to simply open the day:
                the day that looks for
that moment as simple as the whole country
seems once to have been:
                    as if this present
could equal the quiet of a man, after years,
standing to speak at Gettysburg;
                      or months
before, the thoughtless quiet of a bluetick hound
at Milledgeville, lifting an ear to how history arrives.

It is simple to think we ever were simple,
even when we were the boy with the camera, standing
where luck would have us, when a three-horse pumper
rounded a corner in Kankakee.
                Think of whatever morning
it was when Sam Clemens first played hooky in Hannibal,
and thought he might write a book or two
which might finally come to be about
                who we think now
we always thought we wanted to be.

SNAPSHOT

Ten years married, never
an affair; how easily honest
I looked, how naturally easy
about myself, or the world I
believed was about me.
Poised there in blue air
on the edge of the planet,
jawline taut, pipe lit, how
sure I was what it all,
in general, meant. I come back
to myself in sharp focus:
exposed, processed, returned
in a self-addressed envelope:
a transparent boy, a bony
young father. The contrasts
still hold: nothing has faded
that clean illusion of self-
possession. Now I know less,
and better: I've grown less lean,
less easily pleased: I'm tenderer,
harder, angry at all I've
not become; I'm more worn,
more generous, more strangely
myself. And more horny.

PUBLIC BROADCAST

Sunday, late. The winter dark already coming down.
Inside the woodshed door, an early FM tuned to Bangor.
Half as old as the backyard oak he's felled—felled,
fitted, split—an old man mad for music lugs the chunks in.
He turns the volume up, up full: an opera he never saw
rises through light snow and marshalls its triumphant march.
He marches, lifting stiff knees into highstep, marking
his own bootprints, shooting his victorious fist
against a stand of second growth ranked naked
against the sky. He lets the music take him as
he assumes the music: entering the city gates
he feels the blaze of banners, the shine on breastplates
and the women's hair. He marches near the column's head,
in his just place. The sun on the lead car is hot,
the horses sweat with victory, a victory
he hasn't felt in fifty years. Measure upon measure,
the music pumps him higher. He marches, marches,
through his deep backyard. The chorus soars:
the women's voices open every street, their smiles
are wide with glory, their lips already moist.

DREAMBOAT

Wanting a boat, making the rounds
of boatyards, grounding the dream
of having her, figuring costs,

tying one on at the jazz hole
down by the wharf, as high
as Sea Smoke on *China Boy*;

Taiwan cutters junky with teak,
but Julie (all of eleven last Tuesday),
her father at sea, dancing out

in the street with her mother,
a dreamboat rigged like
a yawl called *Concinnity*;

maybe it's time to order another,
to hoist a few more, over old
Muskrat Ramble, over the blues,

wanting a hull with good sheer
and fine entry, her lines
fair as the riff of the heart

within the crest and lift
of the music, the band surging
on *Maple Leaf Rag,* Julie feeling

her body feel it, the lead trumpet
riding it out, the mind blowing solo
out across the Atlantic.

GANGLIA

As long as you
know you don't know,
not knowing's not
what hurts,
               it's what
you don't know you
don't know that
finally gets
to you, right
in the old
solar plexus.

PARTING

That you are moving so far
will not, as you say,
tear me apart; it is having

to part that tears at
my being, that takes part
of me with you against

all reason, against your will,
against mine; you have
every reason to go, but

that you are going, going
away so far, changes
the map: already I have

in mind the whole city,
not merely your building,
become a crater, a circle

surrounding nothing—
and cast out from it, from
the explosion, a shadow

lengthened into the actual
desert, time zones beyond
today's sunrise, where I

am already flying out
toward you, down to
that shadow's thin end,

down the map to where
you, not yet gone, have already
taken me with you, moved

as I am to find that you
are actually going, going
so far as to prove, beyond

all saying, that in this
irrefutable world it is not
love by which we're torn apart.

CYCLE

Stretching his ankles into high gear,
the man commanding ten speeds pumps up
his heart and lowers his head against

the north rain. He's riding into November,
miles from where he intended, years
from where he has been. Downhill now,

he steadies himself on curves by how
the thin wheels gyroscope; he leans
to feel speed, losing weight as

he settles his butt to pedal across
the flats and outside the old suburbs.
Once he's left the suck of traffic

the gravity of the hills gets to him:
he slows to how oaks cantilever,
how spruce true themselves at right angles

against the sky. Gut, heart, toe, knee:
over and over he keeps instructing his body
not to forget: this pumping is toward new country.

PROCESSION

A white-throat flicked into the sunset window.
How small a thing to bury: his short neck limp,
eye perfectly blank, the feathers warm in my hand.

Nothing left now to whistle *Old Sam Peabody,
Peabody, Peabody.* . . . The rest in their thickets,
knowing to go. The winter stars coming. Out early

this morning I see Orion, the first time this fall,
Aldebaran brilliant in Taurus, the Dipper's
handle tipped down toward daybreak. As sun-up

dims Venus, I walk the first frost out into ground fog,
as it happens. Slowly, it comes to me: today
would be father's 85th birthday. I hear

today's birds in the cedars, woken, knowing to go.
I think of a boy years beyond me, back in Council Bluffs,
a boy with father's name, out on a third-floor porch

after midnight, without knowing why, watching (he must
have told me hundreds of times) against his own horizon
these same winter stars beginning to show.

A MAN IN MAINE

North. The bare time.
The same quick dark
from Rutland to Nome,

the utter chill.
Winter stars. After
work, splitting birch

by the light outside
his back door, a man
in Maine thinks what

his father told him,
splitting outside
this same back door:

every November, his
father said, he thought
when he split wood

of what his father
said the night he
right here died: just

after supper, his
father said, his father
came out back, looked

out at the sky
the way he had
for years, picked up

his ax, struck
the oak clean, and
was himself struck

down; before he
died he just had
this to say:

this time of
year the stars
come close some fierce.

SMALL TOWN

You know.
           The light on upstairs
before four every morning. The man
asleep every night before eight.
What programs they watch. Who
traded cars, what keeps the town
moving.
           The town knows. You
know. You've known for years over
drugstore coffee. Who hurts, who
loves.
           Why, today, in the house
two down from the church, people
you know cannot stop weeping.

BEYOND EQUINOX

The sailboats hauled, their seasonal moorings
towed to mudflat coves; the summer cottages
closed and boarded. Beyond equinox, the short days
let their light back into native lives.
                                  White clapboard
clean as November, the strict lawns raked;
sunset angles again to the granite foundations.
Then months of wind: all day out of the North,
all night with the weight of cold behind it.
Behind Bucksport a partridge buries her ruff
in first snow, and settles in.
                            Up in black dark
to stoke her woodstove, a Water Street widow
turns on the light. She feels how her body has,
by her clothes, been slighted, how her house
no longer fits. Taking her bearings with all
due caution, carefully she thinks to herself:
Where are we when we think? With no one to answer
she speaks aloud: *Inside ourselves, looking out
for our lives.*
                      As the fire catches, her housecat wakes.
Morning keeps coming: the harbor out the window
clears to new whitecaps. Daylong, watching, she
and her cat move from room to room with the sun.

A LIFE

As quick as a hawk's wing tipped
to miss my windshield,
                        I heard myself
swerve my cry
                as she sideslipped into
a hardwood grove:
                        six years now:
                                        her wings
still lift and touch me as
she sails all the way through.

BURNING THE TENTS

It's repulsive at first: the sheer weight
of their numbers, how they gather themselves
along roadsides and fields near the river.
Until one gets used to it, the burning, too,
disconcerts. The tents smoke, their bodies
blacken and smell as they shrivel and fall.
But the torch is almost instant; a true
improvement. Watching them, the little ones first,
the young climbing for cover, the old
simply writhing, one thinks back to
flame pulsed into the bunkers on Iwo.
Or to the old burial pits in Poland.
One feels, at first, for the individuals
trying to escape. And some, of course, do.
But the hand-held torch is, for a fact,
clean: one learns to scorch the survivors
almost by rote. The least of them
would return to lay waste to the land.
Their numbers are fearsome. Five million
might be well within range. Against them,
one learns to admit how much he respects
the torch. Just before supper tonight
a friend of mine with another outfit
dropped by, and wanted to try ours out.
He waded out into them, grinning, said
they reminded him of *all them goddamned Chinese*.
And when he came back in to have supper,
still grinning, he saluted, said *Yessir,*
that jesusly torch sure does pucker them up.

FIRE ON THE ISLAND

People, on their safe shore, two miles
away, look out at the island as if
they were wondering what it all meant.
As if, if they knew how it started,
the fire might end like a poem they once
tried to learn: *Water, water,*
everywhere. . . . But nobody knows
how it started. Everyone asks. But
then they get back to *Nobody knows.*
Maybe the corner behind the old stove.
Or sun, through a bullseye bottle
focused on an old couch. Who can tell?
Whatever happened, there it is:
the smoke plumed, the flame grown, until
even the mainland can see it, two miles
away. Now the whole side of the house,
the old gray shingles catching,
fire climbing the trellis where once
there must have been roses. Next to
the woodshed, now, the dead spruce
become a huge torch. Now the whole house,
the fire beginning to top. The way
the wind is, the whole island.
The whole island, for sure. *For*
sure, they say on the mainland,
the way people say. *But what*
can you do, they keep saying.
A schoolkid keeps wanting to know
Why don't they try to save it?
A girl who's getting ready for
college has barely started to say
No way when the whole sky
over the island blows. Maybe only
a propane tank, maybe some stored
explosive. Whatever it was,
there's a different smoke. But no
sound at all, on the mainland.

The way the wind was, the report
must have blown out to sea.
Jesus, an old man says, *she's
gone for good now.* The girl
half hugs herself: *That really
blew me away. I mean it could.
It could blow you away. And . . .*
Already the sky looks half clear.
No, the old man says, *no And.
Right there's the whole of it.*
But nobody knows for sure
what the whole of it means.
However it started, or whatever
blew, there's no telling now
whose words began to come close.
Whatever they once were wondering,
the people have all gone into
their houses. The island is where
it always was, alive in
its own low smouldering.

SPECIES

For seasons beyond count, age
after age, through generations,
they watched us, naked of eye,

through every possible lens:
we were pictured, widely, as
of more or less intelligence.

They measured our migrations,
guessed at the code in our blood,
the tidal pull of the sun,

or what the stars told us.
In weather when we spoke clearly
what they only partially sensed,

they knew to tape our voices;
they collected how they thought
we spoke. Or sang. Of how

we spoke they wrote music.
To our habitats, fieldmarks, even
our habits of pairing, they made

themselves guides. They saw
in us an endangered species;
they listed us with governments.

Out of guilt for the hunting,
even long after, or for what
we barely reminded them of,

we believe they almost loved us.
What we can never know is
how we failed to let them feel

what we meant in our deepest instinct,
in the great dance of our silence.
At the latitudes where we winter,

we only know to gather, to sing
to our young and ourselves, warning
after warning of how they became extinct.

OVER ANTARCTICA

So. After years of plans and logistics,
here we are finally: at the high latitudes

far to the South, running low on everything,
but otherwise setting some kind of record,

flying a not small plane against the spin
of the planet. We circumnavigate close

to the pole, close to what we dreamt
as its infinite stillness. It's gone,

whatever it was: the dream, the world,
the dream of a world; it's as much lost to us

as we are to it. Over and over, as we
home in on an absence, the instruments spin:

we swirl and churn in our own debris,
from Point No Point back to Point No Point.

WHERE TIDE

The afternoon almost gone. The tide
at a certain stage of its changing.
The shore giving way to the tide,

the day giving way toward week's end.
Between us and the sea: an inlet
too small to wade, a clump of marshgrass,

a sandspit about to be flooded.
Behind us, a steep summer field.
Our backs braced against riprap,

we sat facing the tide, the tide
of the light as it capped small waves
and angled into our faces, deepening

as the tide flooded and the light ebbed.
All this was certain. The planet,
not an infinite place, kept

turning on its accustomed axis. We
were another matter, not altogether
apart, but having to face,

in each other's face, how we had
in ourselves faced change. Who,
beyond us, could say what happened;

what part of ourselves could we tell?
We were tidal; where tide measured,
we watched light dull and fog come.

A loon called out of the fog. We heard
another. Of ourselves we could make
no song. We only knew, beyond us,

how light came over the spit,
how fog came over the light, and
how the inlet broadened. After

we'd said as much as we could,
we waded up into the dark
of the still steep field behind us.

STONINGTON

Fog come over us.
Come under sea wind
over cold tide, fog

blown home against
the sharp ebb. Fog
at the harbor bell.

Fog on the headland.
Fog in the goldenrod,
fog at the fishwharves,

come over the island.
Fog tall in spruce,
feeling inland; a soft

quiet on porches, fog
after dark; in small bedrooms,
the harbor bell close.

Spruce full of fog,
fog all this night,
come over all of us.

TABLE

Before he died, he thought,
he might let someone know
how his own life felt;
                but when he looked
to turn out the light, he saw
on his table how things, by way
of his own unwritten will, had already
arranged themselves:
                a photograph of
his wife some forty years since;
                the standard editions
of what he took to be Thoreau's and Melville's
prime hymns; a taped-up paperback called
Character and Opinion, which half-explained
almost everything;
                his own spiral-bound dreamlog
(its tonight's entries still wanting);
a radio, after hours of Bach,
pretuned to tomorrow's weather;
                a marked copy
of Valéry's *Aesthetics;* the portable
Chekhov; and a first-draft poem of the poet
whose work most touched him.
                He had the presence
of mind to leave these matters
as they self-presented.
                He slept
with helical dreams, and woke at first light
to hear rain on the roof, to watch
the scud of low nimbus,
                and then to focus-in
as he reached to the table for
his bifocals:
                to find again in the still life there
an issue of something more than itself,
the more and other that over and over
recalled him, the other and all
to which he woke beholden:

                    and this day
meant again to try to give thanks to, if
he could, for the life of him, join, and return,
any words that might measure.

SAYING IT

Saying it. Trying
to say it. Not
to answer to

logic, but leaving
our very lives open
to how we have

to hear ourselves
say what we mean.
Not merely to

know, all told,
our far neighbors;
or here, beside

us now, the stranger
we sleep next to.
Not to get it said

and be done, but to
say the feeling, its
present shape, to

let words lend it
dimension: to name
the pain to confirm

how it may be borne:
through what in
ourselves we dream

to give voice to,
to find some word for
how we bear our lives.

Daily, as we are daily
wed, we say the world
is a wedding for which,

as we are constantly
finding, the ceremony
has not yet been found.

What wine? What bread?
What language sung?
We wake, at night, to

imagine, and again wake
at dawn to begin: to let
the intervals speak

for themselves, to
listen to how they
feel, to give pause

to what we're about:
to relate ourselves,
over and over; in

time beyond time
to speak some measure
of how we hear the music:

today if ever to
say the joy of trying
to say the joy.

AFTER THE REBUILDING

After the rebuilding was done, and
the woodstove finally installed, after
the ripping-out of walls, tearing back to
its beams the house he'd lived in, frozen, for over
fifty years, he started mornings up with the world's
most expensive kindling. Not just scraps of red oak from
new flooring, ends of clear birch from kitchen trim, and
knots from #2 pine, but oddlot pieces of his old life:
window frames clawed from his daughter's lost room,
his grandfather's coat peg, shelving his mother
had rolled her crust on, and lathing first plastered
the year Thoreau moved to Walden. The woodstove itself
was new: the prime heat for four new rooms descended
from seven, the central logic for all the opening up,
for revisions hammered out daily, weeks of roughing-in,
and after months of unfigured costs, the final bevels
and the long returning. Oh, when he first got up to
rekindle the fire of November mornings, he found
that everything held heat: he sweat as he tossed
the chunks in; he found himself burning, burning.

PRIME

I've been up since black dark, woken again
to Orion's tipped sword, drifted toward
words, thinking beyond constellations to

my dead father, lying abed under his ripped
quilt, trying to warm enough to get to
ablutions, and to stoke both woodstoves;

as soon as the sun turns up, and Sylvia opens
down over the hill, I walk down to loosen myself,
and to listen my share of third-coffee talk:

Harman's last word out the door before Ormy
takes off to pour footings, and Ivan lugs in
the papers, and I climb back to this high bedroom

that looks through bared elms at the tideglint,
and find myself a glad damn fool: trying to even begin
to say how today I love this morning life.

CREATURES

Out of season, a weather
                   calm beyond forecast,
a day high with sun; over
                   the city a sky beyond
belief. On the wooded knoll
                   now a park, above
the river that was always
                   a river, children wander,
kids nibble, lovers
                   meet and part; the old
climb old paths slowly,
                   gaining what once were ramparts
before a rich man
                   built a museum. On the parapet
edging the herb garden,
                   a young woman leans to
her son and says, without
                   pointing, *Look at
that sky. That must be
                   the color of Kingdom Come.*
A man who looks Dutch
                   asks his wife to translate
just as the mother asks
                   him to take her camera to
take her photograph with
                   her son. The wife, in
dubious French, says
                   *Le ciel a une couleur
de fin du monde.* The mother
                   smiles, *Mais non, peut-être
d'un monde meilleur.* They laugh
                   as the mother, thinking
I'm with them, hands me
                   the camera; I take two pictures:
first the mother and son,
                   then, as they change position,
I try to get all of them in.

Inside, blinded first
                    by the dark, then the deep light of
the tapestries, I stand
                    in line, passing what before I had known
only second hand;
                    passing each hanging now next to
the Dutch or French
                    couple, after the son and mother, before other
strangers, passing
                    slowly, until I come to the seventh and,
beyond logic, to tears.

Oh, that this creature
                    should come to be hunted.
And wounded, fenced,
                    chained: linked by the neck
to the tree in a field
                    wild with flowers, flowers
we know still, a tapestry
                    of our earliest seasons.
He and the flowers, he
                    and the tree, they are all
but equal, yet he
                    is prime: in infinite patience
how high his eye gazes,
                    how long his neck holds.
And his wounds—
                    that one of our kind, not for once
but for all, should so attack him—
                    how the small blood
drips from his side, how
                    carefully he lies in the flowers
we know still: iris and
                    daisies, columbine, bluets,
and red and gold blooms
                    beyond number or name. How can it be
this late in the world
                    we also have come to hunt ourselves,
ourselves in this creature,
                    to hunt him in us. He lets us

close in: he allows us to see
              that in him we are met, met with
a resurgent joy,
          a joy in the world we walk back into
no one of us
        must let ourselves destruct.

WHERE WE FIND ROOM

To give to how life takes us:
                         to reach each other
down into, or through, a stillness
that moves like music:
                         say the chromatic scale of hills
as one comes over the Carolina blues of Mount Airy,
with its Exxon pumps perched on an outside curve,
and from Fancy Gap, Virginia, pitches down into
the Shenandoah Valley:
                         a deep insistence, a morning
opening North all day: with no reservations to hold ourselves to,
we tell ourselves self-myths we've both sung all our lives;
as long as the sun arcs behind us, even in silence
we hear each hear the other.
                         Just east of Carlisle,
as its neons go on to compete with sunset,
we finally pull in:
                         the whole fool motel is overextended:
in floodlit lots at the ends of multiple ells, off-duty cops
patrol a classic convocation of Chevys, their chromes
a lightshow beside our blue Rabbit:
                         unpacking, I hear
the cops' jazz: '55 Bel Air ragtops, the first
OHV V–8; a '56 Nomad wagon, the finny '57's:
double-speared hoods, fender skirts, Dagmars, and
four-barrel carbs. Hundreds of classics, a lot two-tone,
blaring back at the motel neon,
                         their licenses
from all over New England, both Virginias, Ohio,
Delaware, Jersey, New York;
                         last night the Blue Ridge,
tonight the world: O truly tonight the world
has come to Jim Thorpe's hometown!
                         We sip Jim Beam
in the ice of our room, watching the President lisp
on the color screen with the sound tuned out, watching
real-life TV out the soundless window: fathers become new masters

of beer and restoration, moms nursing rum cocktails, watching over
their kids, black-and-white in the pool's choppy seas.

                                                        In time
we may be here again, or we once were before; or
just come over a different divide, far from the Carolinas,
we're almost who anybody might be:

                                     just settled, coolly together,
scanning magazine ads, half-watching the TV change to
a man appearing to upstage a temple
as he talks about a native of Samos
until he gives in to a hymn of great names:

                                       Hipparchus,
Euclid, Dionysus of Thrace,

                             Archimedes,
Ptolemy . . .

                O what a wonder their wondering is!
                What is man that we are part of being?
                That we should hear the universe in us,
                that we, this night, are nowhere if not here:

                                       each
and each,

                come by no map to where we find room, let down into
evening, giving toward tears or love, here
where the world much isn't yet most assuredly is,

                                  recalling already
how all day we traveled: to music we made or heard,
almost as now we hear it still,
almost all by ourselves.

EVENING

Evening: the fog rides in over small woods,
unrolling onto the garden made from the field.

In the house, the boy who planted the garden
takes his turn at putting together supper. The father,

who rented the house to have his time with the boy,
picks volunteer phlox by the edge of the woods.

The fog feels like rain, the garden needs sun. The boy
sets the table with spoons, then tosses three kinds

of lettuce, chopped scallions, spinach, and lots
of sliced cucumbers into a bowl. He passes his father

the ketchup. They sit on the two chipped chairs without
saying the blessing; the flowers the father put in a jar

grace the table. They have another week left.
Except for having to finish the postcard he's almost

written his mother, the boy is happy. Watching him
pour more ketchup onto his salad, his father

invents another new face. The boy grins.
His father points to the postcard; he washes up

by himself while the boy writes his mother.
Then his father reads the next chapter he promised.

The fog is all but asleep in the woods, evening
deepens the house; August has settled over the garden

the man and his son dug in June from the field.

THE GARDEN: PENOBSCOT BAY

When we dug them
last fall—the Kennebecs,
Green Mountains, Red
Pontiacs—the rows were
hilled softly where

we had earlier
hoed them, the potatoes
big and clean in October's
light earth. Now, May,
a late spring with cold

rain, the garden we go
to the shore to turn over
is mulched with volunteer
stones, the scattered moraine
left stranded by last

winter's thaws and thousands
of years of glaciers:
the garden become—in
every raw gorge and sharp
drumlin—a deep

relief map of the ledges
and islands out in
the Bay that are, on
a good day, our year-
round best crop.

NORTH HAVEN

Two old friends, dead too early.
September. And then May. Now
here, July, high mid-
                    July: the lettuce
tidal with dew, the hedge grown tall
with cedar waxwings. A ruby-throat holds
in mid-air,
                    sipping long at the feeder.
Given death, our fortune is to
live the life the dead left without words,
to take as given that the boats are in,
the first crop hay.
                    High season
is where we've arrived: bright
as white paint on white clapboard,
the sun becomes our custom:
                    clean of dreams,
we climb out of sleep into weather:
eased from fog, we take ourselves
for a morning dip. And stay
and stay to swim:
                    every day
we stay we keep on arriving: here
or nowhere, tide on tide, we have time
to accept:
                    we have the weather,
we have our lives: to days
like these we have ourselves to give.

A TWO INCH WAVE

The sea, flat
          on a coming tide:
a two inch wave
               climbs the low sand,
drags, curls,
          and topples.
Over and over,
             the water toppling
gathers and
          gains on itself.
It tempts us,
          whoever it is
we think we are,
          to humanize
comparisons
          —but that belongs
to another
          century's nonsense.
Only the semi-
          palmated plovers,
feeding in mid-
          migration, two
strong, claim
          the advancing edge
as their own:
          they dip quick beaks
at something
          we cannot pretend
to see;
          inshore of ducks
floating calm,
          off-tide of oaks
growing tall,
          between the field
of a field
          and the field of the
incoming sea,

                    they dip quick beaks
into a margin
                    we cannot fathom;
they strike for
                    a sustenance only
they know. We
                    only partially
guess. The planet,
                    maybe
the cosmos,
                    they share with us,
or we share
                    with them, is a mystery
not to be solved;
                    what is here, now,
is *here, now,*
                    beyond every knowledge
except our caring:
                    fetched from behind
the old sun,
                    in the huge blue over us still,
Arcturus and all
                    her proximate stars
are already bound
                    to brighten and seem
to rise, as they
                    even now tip to ebb,
angled into the sea
                    on their own inviolate wavelength.

RELATIONS:
OLD LIGHT/NEW SUN/POSTMISTRESS/EARTH/04421

From broken dreams,
                    we wake to every day's
brave history,

the gravity
          of every moment
we wake

to let our lives
               inhabit: *now, here, again,*
this very day,

passionate as all
                 Yeats woke in old age
to hope for, the sun

turns up, under
              an offshore cloudbank
spun at 700 and

some mph to meet it,
                    rosy as the cheeks
of a Chios woman

Homer may have been
                   touched by, just
as Janet

is touching, climbing
                     familiar steps, granite
locally quarried,

to work at 04421,
                 a peninsular village
spun, just as

Janet is spun,
             into light, light appearing

to resurrect

not simply its own
    life but the whole
improbable

system, tugging
    the planet around to
look precisely

as Janet looks,
    alight with the gravity
of her office,

before turning
    the key that opens up
its full

radiance:
    the familiar arrivals,
departures,

and even predictable
    orbits in which,
with excited

constancy, by how
    to each other
we're held, we keep

from spinning out
    by how to each other
we hold.

ACKNOWLEDGMENTS

Thanks to the editors of the following journals and presses for first printing these new poems, some in versions now slightly revised:

"A Fire on the Island," "Burning the Tents," "Relations," "Stonington," "Where We Find Room," *The American Poetry Review;* "To Think," *The American Scholar;* "A Life," *The Amicus Journal;* "Small Town," *Choomia;* "The Garden: Penobscot Bay," "A Man in Maine," *The Country Journal;* "Prime," *Crazyhorse;* "Evening," "Table," "Where Tide," *The Georgia Review;* "Public Broadcast," *The Harvard Magazine;* "A Two Inch Wave," "Procession," *The Hudson Review;* "Here, There," *The New England Review/Bread Loaf Quarterly;* "After the Re-building," *The New Yorker;* "Ganglia," "Over Antarctica," "Species," *The Ontario Review;* "Beyond Equinox," *The Palaemon Press;* "Dreamboat," *Pequod;* "North Haven," *Ploughshares;* "Creatures," "Saying It," *Poetry;* "Cycle," "Parting," *Poetry Northwest;* "Snapshot," *Three Rivers Poetry Journal;* "Growing Up in Kankakee," *TriQuarterly.*

I also want to acknowledge that lines 29 and 30 of "Saying It" owe to Delmore Schwartz's title, as well as to his own source, the Talmud; the questions of line 34 I hear as resonating not only with familiar Christian sources, but specifically with Wallace Stevens' poem "The American Sublime." The italicized question in "Beyond Equinox" is the subject, and title, of the fourth section of Hannah Arendt's *Thinking,* the first volume of *The Life of the Mind.*

Thanks to the National Endowment for the Arts, and to The Academy of American Poets, for the substantial fellowships that enabled me to begin new work and to complete this book. I most of all thank my wife, Margaret, Jay Meek, Jo Ann Fineman, Mary McCarthy, James West, Hayden Carruth, Judith Wechsler, and Benson Snyder for longterm criticism and encouragement.

P.B.
Castine, Maine, 1985